the baby
healthy eating
planner

the baby
healthy eating
planner

The easy-to-follow guide
to a balanced diet for
0-1-year-olds, with more
than 250 recipes

Bounty
Books

Baby Healthy Eating Planner
by Amanda Grant

The *Baby Healthy Eating Planner* is meant to be used as a general reference guide and recipe book. While the author believes the information and recipes it contains are beneficial to health, the book is in no way intended to replace medical advice, which you should obtain from a state-registered dietitian, paediatrician or health visitor. You are therefore urged to consult your health-care professional about specific medical complaints.

First published in Great Britain in 2003 by Mitchell Beazley, an imprint of Octopus Publishing Group Limited.
This edition published 2005 by Bounty Books, a division of Octopus Publishing Group Limited, 2–4 Heron Quays, London E14 4JP

ISBN 0 7537 1258 X
ISBN13 9780753712580

A CIP catalogue record for this book is available from the British Library.

While all reasonable care has been taken during the preparation of this edition, neither the publisher, editors, nor the authors can accept responsibility for any consequences arising from the use thereof or from the information contained therein.

Commissioning Editor: Rebecca Spry
Executive Art Editor: Yasia Williams, Christine Keilty
Design: Miranda Harvey
Editor: Diona Gregory
Consultant Nutritionist: Tanya Carr, Fiona Hunter
Special Photography: William Reavell
Front Jacket Photographs: William Reavell and Tara Fisher
Stylist: Juliet Harvey
Home Economy Assistant: Sibilla Whitehead
Production: Alexis Coogan
Index: John Noble

Typeset in Praxis
Printed and bound by Toppan Printing Company in China

Acknowledgements: Thank you to the paediatric dieticians, health visitors, midwives and nutritionists for their invaluable contributions to this book, especially to Victoria Morris (paediatric dietician), Tanya Carr (dietician and consultant nutritionist) and Wendy Robertson RGNRM. Thank you to Sibilla Whitehead, who helped me throughout with research, testing recipes and lots of support, to Kate Andrews for help with recipe testing, to Bill Reavell for photographing 'another' baby book, to Miranda Harvey for a beautiful book design, to Juliet Harvey for beautiful props and to Becca, with whom I adore working – thank you all so much for all your efforts.

To all my friends in Lewes and their new babies who were born while I was writing this book, especially to Nancy, Lily and Gregory

information about this book

recipe symbols:
● The symbols used for each nutrient are for visual identification only; they do not imply that your baby can eat the food shown in that symbol.
● The "also rich in" symbol (see page 6) indicates that a portion of a dish contains more than 25 percent of your baby's daily requirement of the listed nutrients.

recipes:
● All baby portion sizes are approximate, based on the age group of the chapter, and the points listed are based on the stated portion size. However, all babies appetites are different.
● Wash all fruit and vegetables that have not been peeled.

points system:
● The points system is only intended to be a guide.
● If you are successfully breastfeeding, assume as a guide that your baby is consuming the same number of points of each nutrient as is provided by the recommended amount of formula milk.

nutrition:
● The "most recently published recommended nutrient intakes" refer to the British Government's Recommended Nutrient Intakes (RNIs).

Note: The fresh recipes in this book are mostly suitable for the whole family. The frozen recipes are often not suitable for adults, but you can make big batches of them for freezing.

contents

6   **how to use this book**

8   **baby nutrition**
10   why nutrition matters
12   first nutrition
20   why milk is crucial
24   food purity
27   first cooking
28   first kitchen

30   **0-3 months**
32   what's happening to your baby
33   your routine
37   troubleshooting

38   **4-6 months**
40   what's happening to your baby
41   which nutrients are key
42   the weaning process
44   foods to eat and foods to avoid
45   daily food intake
46   your routine
47   troubleshooting
48   sample 4-6 month meal planners
50   fresh breakfasts
54   quick bites: breakfasts
56   breakfasts to freeze
60   fresh savouries
66   quick bites: vegetable purées
68   savouries to freeze
74   fresh pudings
78   quick bites: fruit purées
80   puds to freeze

84   **7-9 months**
86   what's happening to your baby
87   which nutrients are key
88   second stage weaning
90   foods to eat and foods to avoid
91   recommended daily intake
92   your routine
93   troubleshooting
94   sample 7-9 month meal planners
96   fresh breakfasts
100   quick bites: breakfasts
102   breakfasts to freeze
106   fresh savouries
112   quick bites: savouries
114   savouries to freeze

120   quick bites: finger foods
122   fresh puddings
126   quick bites: puddings
128   puddings to freeze

132   **10-12 months**
134   what's happening to your baby
135   which nutrients are key
136   third stage weaning
138   daily food intake
139   foods to eat and foods to avoid
140   your routine
141   troubleshooting
142   sample 10-12 month meal planners
144   fresh breakfasts
148   quick bites: breakfasts
150   breakfasts to freeze
154   fresh lunches
158   quick bites: lunches
160   lunches to freeze
164   fresh suppers
170   quick bites: suppers
172   suppers to freeze
178   quick bites: finger foods
180   quick bites: snacks
182   fresh puddings
186   quick bites: puddings
188   puds to freeze

190   index

How to use the charts and symbols

During the first year of your baby's life, five nutrients are particularly important: protein, iron, zinc, calcium, and vitamin C. The "nutrients per day" chart opposite illustrates how I have converted the most recently published recommended nutrient intakes (see "nutrition" on page 4), which are usually measured in grams (g), milligrams (mg) or micrograms (mcg), into points for each of these nutrients. Where the recommended daily nutrient intake does not convert exactly to points, I have rounded it up to the nearest quarter or half point. All my recipes have icons illustrating how many points of each of these nutrients a single portion of the dish contains. So, using the "nutrients required per day" charts (see opposite) as easy reference, you can count up the points for each nutrient that you've fed your baby in a day to check if he is getting the required amount. To help you further, points are calculated for three stages: 4-6 months, 7-9 months, and 10-12 months.

Of course, you must also ensure that your baby has a sufficient intake of the other important nutrients: saturated and unsaturated fats, carbohydrates (starch and sugar), vitamins A, D, E, and B group, and the mineral phosphorous. However, as long as he's enjoying a varied diet, he's likely to be getting enough of all of these nutrients. But on pages 16-19 you'll find a guide to how much of each of these nutrients your baby needs and lists of which foods contain them. Recipes that are rich in one or more of these nutrients (apart from fats and carbohydrate) feature an icon (see below and "recipe symbols" on page 4).

how to use
this book

The most important thing to remember is that this points system is designed to be used as a guide. Do bear in mind that many babies will need less than the recommended nutrient intake that the "nutrients required per day" charts refer to, but a small minority will need slightly more – if in doubt, ask your health visitor. Some days your baby will exceed the recommended nutrient intake and other days he'll fall short, but it's his average intake over weeks and months that's important. This unique points system will give you a good guide, but if you are ever in doubt about your baby's nutritional intake, always ask the doctor or state-registered dietitian.

symbols

Each recipe in this book features a selection of these symbols. Each of the symbols that represent a nutrient is accompanied by a number to show how many points of that nutrient a portion of the dish contains. The tick symbol shows that a portion of the dish gives more than 25 per cent of the recommended daily requirement of the nutrients listed alongside it.

 protein

 iron

 zinc

 calcium

 vitamin C

 rich in listed nutrient/s

 suitable for babies over 1 year old

nutrients required per day charts

This chart shows how many points of each nutrient your baby needs per day at each age (see pages 41, 87, and 135). While most professionals assess your baby in terms of weight and age, I have used age only in order to simplify matters. Of course, babies' weights will vary, but on the whole this only affects how much they eat rather than the food types that are acceptable for their digestive and immune systems. Weight may, however, have an impact on nutritional requirements; if you have a heavy baby, follow the points system as a guide but slightly increase the amount of food given – this should compensate for any extra nutrients required.

age	protein 1 point = 1.5g	iron 1 point = 1.5mg	zinc 1 point = 1mg	calcium 1 point = 105mg	vitamin C 1 point = 5mg
4-6 months	8½	3	4	5	5
7-9 months	9	5	5	5	5
10-12 months	10	5	5	5	5

how to build a daily meal plan for your baby, based on a 7-9-month-old baby

This shows how to ensure that your baby gets enough nutrients by adding up the points in his daily food. It doesn't matter if the points requirement is exceeded, although you should not excessively exceed the intake.

time	food and milk	protein	iron	zinc	calcium	vitamin C
breakfast	Breast milk/200ml formula	2	1	1	½	2/4
	1 portion vanilla porridge	3	½	1	½	0
mid-am	Breast milk/200ml formula	2	1	1	½	2/4
lunch	1 portion quick pizza	3½	½	½	1	0
	1 portion pear and almond yogurt	3	0	½	1	½
	water	0	0	0	0	0
mid-pm	Breast milk/200ml formula	2	1	1	½	2/4
supper	1 portion sweet potato and coconut curry	1½	½	0	½	2½
	1 portion rice cakes with mango purée	½	0	1	0	3
	water	0	0	0	0	0
bedtime	Breast milk/200ml formula	2	1	1	½	2/4
	Total	19½	5½	7	5	14/22

Good nutrition is vital to help your baby's body to function, grow efficiently and repair itself, and to ensure good health throughout life. Start by giving your baby a broad range of fresh, unrefined and if possible organic foods. In this way you can help to ensure that, by the age of 12 months, he will be eating a well-balanced and healthy diet.

As babies have small appetites, they need small, frequent meals made up of nutrient-dense foods. All foods provide a mixture of nutrients, but no single food, apart from breast milk or formula milk during the first six months, provides them all.

baby
nutrition

why nutrition
matters

"Nutrition in the early years of life is a major determinant of growth and development and it also influences adult health"
The Committee on Medical Aspects of Food Policy "COMA" Report.

By far the best food for your baby in the first few months is breast milk. Ideally, you should try to breastfeed for at least the first 4 months (see pages 20–23). Once your baby reaches the age of 4 months you can start to wean him onto "solid" foods – that is, foods and liquids other than milk (although the foods babies eat at this stage can hardly be described as "solid"). The foods you choose to feed him should be the best foods for his development and growth (see pages 42–43).

your baby's immune system

Your baby's immune system is very immature at birth and it needs to develop to become healthy and strong. The strength of your baby's immune system is dependent on an optimal, balanced intake of nutrients. From birth, the first food to assist in building a strong immune system is colostrum, the liquid that comes from the breast before the milk comes in (see page 20). Colostrum contains many antibodies to combat bacteria and viruses, and so support, your baby's immune system. Colostrum also contains a high concentration of zinc, which is essential for a child's growth and development. Formula milks are fortified with zinc.

your baby's digestive system

Your baby's digestive system is far from being fully developed in his first few weeks of life, which is why breast milk is the perfect food. It can take up to four months for your baby's intestines to develop and to produce the right enzymes for digesting foods. Similarly, his kidneys will not be able to cope with eliminating waste products from solid food. It makes sense that if solid foods are introduced too early, your baby's digestive system may become damaged. This is one of the reasons why babies are usually weaned between 4 and 6 months old and not earlier.

essential nutrients

The reason for making sure that your baby's diet gradually becomes more varied and balanced is because he needs all of the essential nutrients to grow and develop, and to develop strong and healthy immune and digestive systems. His diet needs to be varied, because no one nutrient works in isolation and a severe deficiency of one vitamin or mineral can adversely affect his development.

energy

Energy-dense foods are very important for the first year of life, as your baby's demands for energy are high due to his rapid growth and development while his stomach capacity is small. It is important to remember that standard adult healthy eating advice (low fat, high fibre diets) should not be given to babies or young children under 2 years of age.

fresh fruit and vegetables

Non-citrus fruit and vegetables make great first foods as they are unlikely to cause allergies in babies. They also contain a concentrated supply of vitamins, minerals, trace elements, and beneficial enzymes, which can be quickly absorbed into your baby's system and bloodstream. Enzymes are particularly important for your baby's health as they are essential to every stage of metabolism. They can be destroyed during cooking. At first, breast milk will provide all the essential enzymes your baby needs. After 9-10 months, to supplement your baby's enzyme intake, increase the amount of steamed fruit and vegetables you give so long as your baby is confident with chewing.

the importance of vitamins

I often mention antioxidant vitamins (such as vitamins A, C, and E) in this book and, although we associate these with cancer, heart disease, and problems that generally occur later in life, they also play a significant role in assisting the immune system and enabling the body to maintain health.

the points system

To help make your life easier during these formative months I have chosen five of the key nutrients your baby needs (see page 6) and designed a points system around them. This is intended to help you easily get used to feeding your baby a balanced diet. At the same time, it will reassure you that he is eating the recommended amount of each of these nutrients on a daily basis. There are, however, other nutrients that are also very important during this first year of your baby's life. (To find out how to ensure a healthy intake of all the key nutrients, see pages 12–19.)

first
nutrition

key protein foods

These foods are not all suitable for babies in all age groups. See the relevant chapters for specific advice.

Protein foods providing all the essential amino acids include:
- Meat, such as chicken and lamb
- Fish, such as salmon and tuna
- Dairy products, such as Cheddar cheese and yogurt
- Eggs
- Soya products, such as tofu, soya beans, and soya cheese.

Good vegetarian protein sources include:
(These do not contain all of the essential amino acids. However, in combination they can – for instance, vegetable burgers served with rice.)
- Beans and pulses, such as chickpeas, beans, lentils, and butter beans
- Cereals and grain foods, such as rice, pasta, oats, and nut-free muesli
- Finely ground nuts, such as hazelnuts and almonds, and smooth nut butters (do not give nuts to babies if there is a family history of food allergies).
- Ground seeds, such as sunflower seeds, and sesame seeds.

protein

Protein consists of building blocks called amino acids. There are two types of amino acids: essential and non-essential. Essential amino acids must be obtained directly from food, while the body can produce non-essential amino acids from other sources. Therefore you need to make sure that your baby's diet contains enough essential amino acids (see "key protein foods", left).

why your baby needs it

Protein is one of the most important nutrients for helping the body build and repair muscles, tissues, hair, and organs, and maintain an effective immune and hormonal system. Considering how fast babies grow during their first year, this is definitely one of their key nutrients.

how to make sure your baby gets it

An adequate intake of protein, in particular, should be ensured during weaning. This will be easy to achieve if you aim to feed your baby a diverse diet by the time he is 9 months old. "If your baby is regularly consuming meat, fish, eggs and reasonable quantities of milk he is unlikely to be protein deficient" (UK Department of Health). If you are feeding your baby a vegetarian diet, you do need to pay attention to make sure that he eats enough protein-rich foods. Most plant foods are low in protein compared with foods of animal origin (with the exception of soya products), and the proteins from any single plant, unlike animal proteins, do not contain all the essential amino acids. This is why it is important to feed your baby a mixture of plant foods to help make sure that the complete range of essential amino acids is provided. Mothers wishing to offer their baby a vegan diet should seek specialist advice from a state-registered dietitian.

iron

There are two main types of iron in food – haem iron from lean red meat and non-haem iron from plants sources, such as vegetables, finely chpped dried fruits, and finely ground nuts.

why your baby needs it

Iron is needed for healthy blood and muscles. A lack of iron can lead to a common form of anaemia. A significant number of babies under 12 months do not achieve a good iron intake. It is very rare for babies to get too much of this mineral because they are unable physically to eat large quantities of it. (For example, the RNI for babies 4 to 6 months old is 4.3mg a day; 100g beef provides 3.1mg of iron.)

how to make sure your baby gets it

At birth, babies born at term (as close to 40 weeks as possible) need only a small amount of iron because they have laid down stores that will last them for 6 months.

The level of iron in breast milk is low, but since about 50 per cent or more of it is absorbed – which is a high rate of absorption for iron – this makes an important contribution for your breastfed baby during early weaning. Many formula milk powders are fortified with iron. The amount of iron contributed from breast and formula milk by the time the baby is 6 months old is insufficient to meet his increasing needs.

One of the main functions of weaning is to increase your baby's iron intake. A large number of babies under the age of 12 months do not achieve the recommended level due to late weaning and inappropriate foods.

Babies, like adults, find it easier to absorb haem iron. They are capable of absorbing 20 to 40 per cent of the iron from meat and only 5 to 20 per cent of the iron available from vegetable sources. Consequently, you will need to feed your baby a good variety and quantity of vegetables to provide him with a good supply of iron. The absorption of iron is enhanced by the presence of adequate vitamin C in the diet.

key iron foods

These foods are not all suitable for babies in all age groups. See the relevant chapters for specific advice.

- Red meat, such as beef and lamb
- Eggs
- Beans – including baked beans
- Tofu (a soya bean product)
- Oily fish, such as tuna, mackerel and sardines
- Puréed or finely chopped dried fruits, such as unsulphured apricots, raisins and prunes
- Wholegrain cereals and bread
- Finely ground nuts (do not give nuts to babies if there is a family history of food allergies).
- Green vegetables, particularly broccoli and spinach

Avoid giving your baby foods containing tannin or caffeine as they will inhibit iron absorption.

calcium

Calcium is a mineral needed for strong, healthy bones and teeth.

why your baby needs it

Ninety-nine per cent of the body's calcium content is found in bones and teeth, with one per cent in blood plasma and soft tissues. But calcium is needed during the first year of your baby's life to help with the normal function of all cells as well as for bone and teeth development.

how to make sure your baby gets it

Your baby should quite easily be able to get sufficient calcium if he eats a good range of dairy produce and other calcium-rich foods.

zinc

The mineral zinc has many functions in your baby's body. These include maintaining a healthy immune system and assisting in growth.

why your baby needs it

Zinc deficiency may limit your baby's growth. If your baby is vegetarian, be careful not to feed him too many wholemeal foods because they can adversely affect the absorption of this mineral. Try to feed him low-fibre foods.

how to make sure your baby gets it

A significant number of babies under the age of 12 months do not achieve the recommended daily level of this nutrient from their diet. Meat and meat products are the richest sources of zinc, but these foods contribute only 10 per cent of the dietary zinc intake, so make sure your baby's diet includes other good sources.

vitamin C

Vitamin C is one of the best-known antioxidant vitamins. Antioxidant vitamins are well-known for helping to prevent life-threatening diseases, such as cancer, but they are also particularly good at boosting the immune system.

why your baby needs it

Vitamin C is needed for growth and healthy body tissue and is important in the healing of wounds. Vitamin C also helps with the absorption of iron and 'probably' zinc. This makes it particularly useful to babies fed little or no meat. Breast and formula milk are normally good sources of this vitamin.

how to make sure your baby gets it

It is important to make sure that your baby's diet provides a good combination of both raw and cooked fruits, and cooked vegetables. Vitamin C is very easily destroyed by heat and light, so include raw or very lightly cooked foods in your baby's diet. But remember, babies cannot cope with citrus fruits until they are 6 months old, and you should only serve chunks of fruit and vegetables to babies who are confident with chewing.

key vitamin C foods

These foods are not all suitable for babies in all age groups. See the relevant chapters for specific advice.
- Kiwi fruit
- Strawberries
- Oranges
- Mango
- Papaya
- Raspberries
- Nectarines
- Peaches
- Blackcurrants.
- Red, green, and yellow peppers
- Broccoli
- Spinach
- Cabbage
- Potatoes
- Mange-tout and peas.

fats

Fats and oils are made up of molecules of fatty acids and glycerol. All fats are a combination of three types of fatty acids. A fat is said to be saturated, mono-unsaturated or polyunsaturated, depending on which type of fatty acid is present in the largest proportion. Saturated fats, such as butter, are solid at room temperature and are sometimes referred to as the "bad" fats. Mono-unsaturated, such as olive oil, and polyunsaturated fats, such as sunflower oil, are liquid at room temperature.

why your baby needs them

Energy-dense foods are essential to meet your baby's demands for his rapid growth and development. Foods that contain fats provide not only a concentrated source of energy but also the fat-soluble vitamins A, D, E, and K, all of which are vital in the healthy development of your baby. Some fatty acids in the diet are essential to health. It is this "quality" of fat that is more important than worrying about quantity for this age group. Let your baby's appetite guide you. And remember, low-fat products and diets are not suitable for your baby.

how to make sure your baby gets them

Essential fatty acids are found in plant and fish oils. They cannot be made in the body and so, like vitamins and minerals, they need to be present in the baby's diet. Fat is the greatest provider of energy to babies in the first months of life. More than 50 per cent of the energy from breast milk comes from fat. Infant formula milks and follow-on formula milks provide 30 to 56.6 per cent of their energy from fat.

carbohydrates

There are two types of carbohydrates: simple (sugars) and complex (starches and fibre). They are the body's primary source of energy.

why your baby needs them

Your baby needs a good source of carbohydrates to provide him with energy necessary to grow and develop.

starches and fibre

Starches and fibre can be refined or natural.

how to make sure your baby gets starch and fibre

"Provided energy intake is adequate, the proportion of energy supplied as starch in the weaning diet should increase as the proportion derived from fat decreases" (COMA).

Starch itself is well-tolerated and easily absorbed by babies, so even though it can be bulky, it is relatively easy to ensure that your baby will consume the right quantity. Foods such as cereals, vegetables, and in particular rice starch, are perfect weaning foods for your baby. High-fibre diets are suitable for children under 1 year old.

sugars

Sugars can either be refined or found in a more natural form.

how to make sure your baby gets sugar

Sugars provide energy but have little overall nutritive value. Your baby will find fruit and milk-based products naturally sweet without you needing to add any sugar. Introducing your baby to too many sweet foods at this stage can encourage him to develop a sweet tooth later in life. A little added to the occasional dessert will not hurt, but it really should only be occasional.

key starch foods

These foods are not all suitable for babies in all age groups. See the relevant chapters for specific advice.

Refined starch foods:
- Processed breakfast cereals
- White flour
- Biscuits and cakes
- Baby rice
- White bread.

Natural starch foods:
- Potatoes
- Breakfast cereals, such as nut-free muesli
- Bread
- Sweetcorn
- Root vegetables, such as parsnips
- Finely ground nuts (do not give nuts to babies if there is a family history of food allergies)
- Chickpeas
- Bananas.

key sugar foods

These foods are not all suitable for babies in all age groups. See the relevant chapters for specific advice.

Natural sugar foods:
- Fruit and vegetables
- Full-fat milk.

Refined sugar foods:
- White and brown coloured sugar
- Rusks
- Biscuits, cakes and jellies.

vitamin A

Vitamin A is found in animal products. Betacarotene is a substance found in plant foods and converted by the body into vitamin A.

why your baby needs it

Vitamin A is needed for growth, development, healthy skin and hair, and good vision.

how to make sure your baby gets it

Only a limited number of foods contain vitamin A other than breast milk, infant formula milk or full-fat milk. For this reason, the UK Department of Health still recommends vitamin drops to ensure that babies have an adequate intake, especially those who are still being breastfed after 6 months or taking less than 500ml formula milk a day. Ask your family doctor or health visitor or paediatric doctor for more information.

vitamin B group

The vitamin B complex comprises vitamin B_1 (thiamine), B_2 (riboflavin), B_3 (niacin), folic acid, B_5 (pantothenic acid), B_6 (pyridoxine), and B_{12} (cyanocobalamin).

why your baby needs it

The B vitamins play many roles. They are essential for your baby's metabolism and maintenance of a healthy nervous system. B vitamins help with the digestion of food and convert it into energy, assist in the production of red blood cells, and maintain a healthy brain and immune system, tissue, and hair.

how to make sure your baby gets it

Many foods supply these vitamins as a package. However, babies breastfed by vegan mothers may receive low levels of vitamin B_{12} from the breast milk. Similarly, babies weaned onto vegan diets may be at risk of becoming deficient in vitamin B_{12}.

vitamin D

why your baby needs it

Vitamin D works with calcium and is essential for the normal growth and healthy development of strong bones and teeth.

how to make sure your baby gets it

Few foods contain vitamin D. It is made mainly by the skin in the presence of sunlight. All babies should have at least 30 minutes of fresh air each day. Breast milk contains little vitamin D and breastfed babies rely on their stores at birth and exposure to sunlight to maintain satisfactory vitamin D levels. Infant formula milks are fortified with vitamin D. Some babies may need vitamin D and A supplementation – ask your state-registered dietician, registered paediatrician, or family doctor for more details.

vitamin E

Vitamin E is an antioxidant which has been shown to decrease the risk of some cancers and heart disease.

why your baby needs it

Vitamin E is needed to help develop and maintain strong cells, especially in the blood and nervous system.

how to make sure your baby gets it

Vitamin E is pretty widely available from the diet, including breast milk and infant formula milk.

phosphorus

Phosphorus is a mineral that works in a way similar to calcium.

why your baby needs it

Phosphorus has an important role in releasing energy to drive metabolic processes and also gives rigidity to the skeleton.

how to make sure your baby gets it

About half his phosphorus will come from milk. Phosphorus is present in nearly all foods.

key vitamin D foods

These foods are not all suitable for babies in all age groups. See the relevant chapters for specific advice.

- Oily fish, such as sardines
- Eggs
- Unsalted butter
- Fortified margarine
- Yogurt and full-fat cheese
- Fortified cereals.

key vitamin E foods

These foods are not all suitable for babies in all age groups. See the relevant chapters for specific advice.

- Unsalted butter
- Meat
- Vegetable oils, such as olive, sunflower
- Cereal products
- Finely ground nuts (do not give nuts to babies if there is a family history of food allergies)
- Ground seeds
- Tomatoes and avocados
- Sweet potatoes
- Spinach
- Mangoes
- Egg yolks
- Sardines
- Salmon.

key phosphorus foods

These foods are not all suitable for babies in all age groups. See the relevant chapters for specific advice.

- Full-fat milk
- Bread and cereal products
- Meat
- Chickpeas
- Potatoes
- Yeast extract
- Pumpkin seeds
- Fruit and vegetables
- Finely ground nuts (do not give nuts to babies if there is a family history of food allergies).

why milk
is crucial

breast is best

Breast milk provides all the essential nutrients your baby needs for development during his first six months. From then on, he requires a combination of milk and solids.

Breast milk is the only food naturally designed for your baby, and research studies have suggested that the health benefits of breast milk can be significant and lifelong. My advice would be to at least start by breastfeeding, as some breastfeeding is better than none. Even premature babies who are given breast milk often do better than those given formula milk.

Breastfed babies can be easier to wean because they have had traces of your diet in your breast milk. Breastfeeding has many advantages for you, too – it helps you to get your shape back and it encourages your womb to contract more quickly. Best of all, breastfeeding is practical; it takes little time to do and the milk is always at the right temperature.

Breastfeeding is natural, but it does not necessarily come naturally to many mums. Don't be afraid to ask for help if you are finding it hard. There are books on breastfeeding, as well as organizations that solely provide information on the subject and counsellors trained to help mothers with difficulties. Breastfeeding is encouraged and supported by most baby experts and health professionals, so persevere. I had a difficult time with my firstborn in the first three months and used to dread the next feed, but I sought help with remarkable results.

colostrum

The first liquid that your breasts produce is called colostrum, and this is the perfect nutrition for your baby during his first few days. Colostrum has more protein and vitamins and less carbohydrate and fat than the mature milk that usually arrives between days three and five. Colostrum also provides antibodies that protect your baby's health while he is building up his immune system and developing long-term resistance to infections. There is no artificial equivalent of colostrum, so even the first few days at the breast give your baby a head start.

breast milk

Breast milk is quite different in appearance, texture, and nutritional composition to colostrum. Breast milk provides the balance and concentration of nutrients in a digestible form and it contains enzymes that aid the digestive process. The make-up of milk varies during your baby's feed: "fore" milk is produced at the beginning of the feed, and is high in volume and low in fat; as your baby progresses he will reach the "hind" milk that will help him go for longer between feeds. This is why your baby should drink for a certain amount of time from one breast before being transferred to the next. As a general guide, once your baby is a week old, he should be

key nutrients in milk

	breast milk (100ml)	formula milk (100ml)
energy:		
kilojoule (kJ)	293kj	280–310kj
kilocalorie (kcal)	70kcal	67–74kcal
protein	1.3g	1.4–1.8g
carbohydrate	7g	7.2–9.3g
fat	4.2g	3.3–3.6g
vitamins:		
A	60µg	64–78µg
D	0.01µg	0.9-1.4µg
E	0.35mg	0.4-1.3mg
C	3.8mg	8.2-9mg
K	0.21µg	0-6.7µg
B vitamins:		
B_1 (thiamin)	16µg	40-100µg
B_2 (riboflavin)	30µg	73-150µg
B_3 (niacin)	620µg	760-960µg
B_5 (panthothenic acid)	260µg	270-450µg
B_6 (pyridoxine)	6µg	40-60µg
B_{12} (cyanocobalamin)	0.01µg	0.14-0.2µg
Folic acid	5.0µg	4.9-13µg
minerals:		
calcium	35mg	46-81mg
phosphorus	15mg	26-48mg
zinc	295µg	500-920µg
iron	76µg	650-1300µg
potassium	60mg	64-85mg
sodium	15mg	16-22mg
chloride	43mg	41-43mg
magnesium	3mg	5-7mg
copper	39µg	17-50µg
iodine	7µg	8.1-12µg

Important note: The rate of absorption of nutrients from breast milk is significantly higher than it is from formula milk. This is particularly relevant in relation to micronutrients such as minerals. That means although most infant formula milks contain higher levels of certain nutrients than human milk, your baby will more easily absorb the nutrients in the latter.

g = gram
mg = milligram (one thousandth of a gram)
µg = microgram (one millionth of a gram)

Breastmilk data from COMA report, "Weaning and the Weaning Diet" (1995). Formula milk range taken from the first milks from the following brands: SMA Gold, Hipp Organic, Cow & Gate Premium and Aptamil.

spending 25 to 30 minutes on the first breast before being transferred. Recent studies have found that breastfeeding can optimize brain development and minimize the chances of neurological problems. There is also evidence to suggest that breastfed babies can have higher IQs than bottle-fed babies because of the essential fatty acids and other key nutrients in breast milk.

Breastfeeding also helps to prevent your baby suffering from minor infections, supporting his underdeveloped immune system for as long as it is offered.

allergies

Breast milk is less likely to cause allergies in your baby than formula milks, most of which are based on cow's milk protein. This is particularly true in families with a strong history of food allergies, eczema or asthma. If, however, during breastfeeding, you notice any symptoms such as diarrhoea, vomiting or rashes, or if you have a family history of allergies to food, speak to your family doctor, registered paediatrician or state-registered paediatric dietician.

your diet when breastfeeding

By feeding your baby breast milk you are giving him a varied diet because your diet affects both the flavour and nutritional composition of your milk. This will also help when you introduce solid foods during weaning. It is important that you eat a balanced, varied diet when breastfeeding. You need to eat foods from all the main food groups, providing all of the essential nutrients. Eat small, frequent meals and drink at least 2 litres of water a day. Try to get plenty of rest (easier said than done), especially if this is not your first baby. You may wish to increase the intake of certain vitamins and minerals while you are breastfeeding. Vitamin D supplementation of 10µg per day is often recommended. For more information, ask your family doctor or state-registered dietician.

your diet when breastfeeding

What you eat will directly affect the quality of your milk.

- Try to buy organic versions of the foods you eat most often.
- Eat plenty of foods rich in starch and fibre, such as bread, cereals, and potatoes.
- Eat a good mixture of five fresh fruits and vegetables a day – it's much easier to do than it may sound. A smoothie can be an easy way to eat two or three pieces of fresh fruit.
- Include milk and dairy produce in moderation.
- Eat some fresh meat and fish or alternatives, such as tofu.
- Use fats in your cooking and your food, but where possible, choose unsaturated fats, such as olive oil, and avocados, rather than saturated fats such as butter.
- Try to avoid sugary foods or drinks.
- Keep alcohol and caffeine intake to a minimum. and avoid them just before a feed.

The UK Department of Health recommends that you increase the intake of certain vitamins and minerals while you are breastfeeding; in particular vitamin D supplementation of 10µg is recommended. For more information see my book "Healthy Eating For Pregnancy" (Mitchell Beazley).

why organic

In recent years many people have become concerned about levels of pesticide residues and other by-products of intensive farming, such as antibiotics, that are found in non-organic food. Although these are permitted levels, deemed safe by the UK Government, there has been an increase in the production and consumption of organic food, in which the levels are much lower. So if you wish to choose more organic foods you will certainly consume fewer presticides. However, since the effect on health, if any, is as yet unknown, going completely organic is a personal choice, and many parents find it too expensive. I choose organic for foods we eat most often, such as milk, bread, and potatoes

advantages of breastfeeding for mum

When you breastfeed, your uterus will return to its pre-pregnancy state much faster than if you are not breastfeeding. Hormones are released during feeding which help you relax. Also, you may find it easier to get your shape back because the extra fat your body lays down in preparation for lactation will be used to feed your baby. Some mums believe that breastfeeding relieves long-term pre-menstrual tension.

disadvantages of breastfeeding for mum

I found the one disadvantage of breastfeeding occurred when it was time to return to work and I had to express more milk. There are many ways to cope with this, and the National Childbirth Trust or La Leche League provide excellent information. Some mums have said they find it frustrating that they have to continue to watch what they are eating and drinking, but it is important to eat a well-balanced and varied diet.

bottle-feeding

There will always be some mothers who have to give up breastfeeding or find that it does not suit them and choose to stop. If you really find breastfeeding too difficult, you should not be pressured to continue. It is more important to ensure you and your baby are happy. There is a school of thought that your baby may suffer emotionally if you stop breastfeeding. My mother breastfed me only for the first few days of my life and no one could have had a stronger bond than she and I had.

If you have decided to bottle-feed your baby from day one, your hospital should provide you with ready-made formula milk. When you leave hospital and must choose a brand of formula milk. I would recommend an organic variety to help ensure it does not contain any artificial additives, chemical pesticides or residues, or GM ingredients.

milk substitutes

Breast, formula, and follow-on milks (offered later on) should be the main drinks in the first year. Cooled, boiled tap water may be given in between feeds (cooled, boiled bottled water is safe unless labelled "natural mineral water", in which case it can contain higher concentrations of solutes such as sodium and fluoride). Other drinks, such as diluted fruit juice, should be given only at meal times once you are weaning, in a feeding cup. It is wise to consult your doctor, midwife, health visitor, nurse, state-registered dietician or pharmacist for more information on breast milk alternatives before choosing.

infant formula milks

These provide a sole source of nourishment for babies for the first four to six months. Infant formula milk is more likely to trigger an allergic reaction than human milk because it is based on cow's milk protein. If you have a family history of allergies, seek advice before you start formula milk feeding.

organic infant formula milks

Made with organic ingredients and guaranteed to be GM free.

soya infant formula milks

There are concerns about the long-term health effects of soya-based infant formula, particularly that babies with a risk of allergies may also become sensitive to soya protein. There has only been one study examining long-term implications and, although it did not find any adverse effects, it is recommended (by the British Nutrition Foundation) that soya-based formulas should only be fed to infants on the advice of a doctor or state-registered dietitian.

follow-on milk

Unlike infant formula milks, these are not intended to be a sole source of nutrition but part of a mixed diet. The levels of some nutrients are higher than in human or cow's milk, with a minimum level of iron twice that specified for infant formula milk.

Fresh cow's, goat's or sheep's milk should not be given as a drink to babies under the age of 1. Similarly, soya drinks, other than soya infant formula milk, should not be given during weaning.

food
purity

organic

A baby has a unique and delicate physiology; his digestive system is far more efficient at absorbing food than an adult's. This enables nutrients to be used quickly, but also makes the baby vulnerable to toxins, especially from additives, pesticides, and other chemical residues often found in non-organic food. In addition, a baby's immature kidneys cannot excrete harmful substances efficiently so they circulate around the body for longer. Research has also found that babies are more exposed to these substances than adults because, weight for weight, babies eat larger quantities of a small range of foods, which are often the ones most contaminated with residues, such as bananas and cow's milk.

Organic food is produced without the use of synthetic pesticides, fungicides, fertilizers, and growth hormones. The processing of organic food, is strictly controlled with the aim of retaining the "integrity" of the food so that no added artificial ingredients, preservatives or irradiation are permitted. There are even stricter regulations for baby foods. I'd advise you to list the five foods you most often give to your baby and resolve to buy organic. Staple foods, such as baby rice, wheat products, fruit, and vegetables, are often the worst offenders when non-organic.

Many parents argue that organic food is too expensive. But as its production is becoming more widespread, prices are falling. There are also ways to buy cheaply without compromising on quality: buy seasonally and from local producers rather than expensively packaged supermarket food and your bills will be lower. Buy unprocessed organic foods such as fruit, vegetables, and meat and cook with them at home rather than buying processed versions.

genetically modified foods

As it develops, GM technology seems to provide solutions to many of the problems in world agriculture and food production. However, in recent years a vociferous anti-GM movement has emerged, and is growing all the time. GM foods have never been in the food chain before and no one really knows how they are going to effect it. The true impact of GM on the environment and our health may not be fully realised for many years. All foods containing GM products are now required by British law to be clearly labelled, making it easy for you to decide whether to buy them or not. All organic food is certified non-GM.

additives and preservatives

There are thousands of additives, in the form of preservatives, antioxidants, artificial colourings, artificial flavourings, flavour enhancers, artificial sweeteners, stabilizers, and thickeners. Their sole purpose is to give factory-processed food a longer shelf-life and to make it more palatable. Few additives have any nutritional value. Research is still being carried out into their long-term effects on human health, in particular on babies and toddlers. Recently, the first official study into the link between food colouring and children's tantrums found that colourings induce hyperactive behaviour in 25 per cent of children. Other studies have shown a link between food additives and conditions such as asthma, eczema, allergies, and even behavioural problems in children.

Additives approved for use in the European Union (EU) have an "E-number" allocated to them. There are now approximately 927 approved E-numbers, but there are also many other ingredients that do not have E-numbers but that can still be used in food. Thankfully E-numbers have been banned from use in baby food, but when your child is weaned and begins to eat what the rest of the family eats, he may be exposed to them. The best thing is to try and cut out foods that are high in additives for all the family, and eat home-cooked food as much as possible. It will be beneficial for all of you.

the importance of freshness

There are many reasons why home-cooked food is better for your baby. Most importantly, freshly prepared food will maximize your baby's intake of essential nutrients, especially if it is cooked for the shortest time possible. Food cooked in this way will look, smell, and taste better than convenience food in jars. This will instil in your baby an appreciation of freshly cooked, unprocessed food that will last a lifetime. If you are feeding your family home-made food, you can easily adapt the meal for your baby. And always remember that, despite what advertisers would have you believe, even organic ready-made food will always be inferior to fresh, home-made versions. Even the best baby foods have been processed, cooked, and packaged and will inevitably have lost some of their nutritional value.

While I am obviously an advocate of home-cooked food, at the same time I realize that sometimes it is just not possible to juggle work and family life and still have time to make fresh meals every day. There is a vast range of convenience foods out there and they are not all bad. By choosing carefully and reading labels, you can buy certain things that will save you lots of time and, if you add some fresh ingredients to them, they can make up a useful part of your baby's diet. If you are buying baby food in jars, add a little mashed banana or avocado – something that is quick and won't need cooking, to up the nutrient content.

labels

Most pre-packaged food for babies is strictly regulated, but get into the habit of reading labels. Look out for and avoid, if possible, the following: salt; sugars – dextrose, glucose, fructose, lactose, maltose, honey, and fruit syrups are all forms of sugar; meat or vegetable extracts, which often indicate overprocessing; processed starches, because they often indicate the overuse of water – they are low-nutrient fillers, such as modified cornflour, rice starch, and wheat starch, and they dull the flavour of the food; flavourings – these are unnecessary for babies and only introduce your child to artificial tastes.

first
cooking

Preparing food at home gives you control over what goes into the dish and it is usually cheaper than buying ready-made food. Yet the main advantage is nutritional. How you cook the food will affect its nutrient content. One of the best ways to prepare vegetables for your baby from 9-10 months is to steam them – as long as he is confident with chewing. Give him chunks of steamed vegetables, such as carrots, to get him used to the texture and taste.

steaming and boiling

When you do cook, especially fruit and vegetables, do it for the shortest time needed. If you boil food, only add just enough water to cover, and if a purée needs thinning, use some of the cooking water.

microwaving

Some scientists are concerned about the effect of microwave radiation on food, particularly on its ability to deplete breast milk's disease-fighting capabilities. I have concerns about the health implications of giving babies microwaved food. I do not use a microwave when I cook for my children; I find steaming, baking and boiling are all preferable alternatives.

freezing

It is a good idea to make more home-cooked food than you need and freeze the excess, especially when you weaning. Most purées freeze brilliantly; exceptions include those made with banana or avocado. For fruit and vegetable purées, you just need some sterilized, rubber ice-cube trays and new freezer bags. As your baby gets older, small ramekins are great for freezing baby-sized meals that need to be reheated. But don't freeze a huge amount of purée because your baby will never get through it! All the recipes in the freezer sections of this book have instructions on when to freeze and how to reheat, but there are a few general rules:

- Cool food quickly that is to be frozen.
- Always label and date the food; after a long time its taste and texture will deteriorate.
- Ideally, defrost food in the refrigerator overnight, although for small cubes of purée this is not necessary – just reheat them in a bowl over a pan of boiling water.
- Make sure that food is thoroughly reheated and never refreeze.
- Freeze breast milk for up to a month.
- Freeze food containing dairy produce for up to six weeks.
- Freeze food made only from fruit or vegetables for up to eight weeks.
- Freeze food containing meat and fish for up to three months.

first
kitchen

equipment

If you are breastfeeding, you won't need any kitchen equipment, but as you start to wean your baby from breast to bottle, whether you are using breast milk or formula milk, there are a few basics you will need: bottles, teats and sterilizing equipment (see below). A bottle insulator is useful for transporting milk when you and your baby are out and about, and is also good for night feeds. An expressor is invaluable when you are breastfeeding, as it will enable you to prepare feeds in advance, giving you some independence from your baby. Both manual and electric ones are available. It's worth asking your hospital if they lend out electric ones.

As your baby starts to eat solid food, you will need an unbreakable bowl (plastic), spoons without hard edges and a large supply of bibs. A stainless-steel saucepan is best because non-stick ones are coated in plastic, which can contaminate food. A steamer is also useful, although a metal colander or sieve on top of a wide saucepan, covered with a lid, makes a good alternative. For making purées, I found that a hand-held blender with a detachable blade was quick and easy to clean, and it can travel with you. A mouli or ricer, or even a nylon sieve, will do the job, but it takes longer. Rubber ice-cube trays are the best for freezing small quantities of baby food, and you'll also need airtight containers and ziplock bags for freezing.

hygiene

Most kitchen hygiene is common sense, but with a baby you will need to take extra care.
● Always wash your hands before preparing feeds and, as your baby becomes old enough to hold food or feed himself, wash his hands before and after meals.
● Make sure all your equipment is clean and sterilized correctly (see below).
● Put raw meat and fish at the bottom of the refrigerator, ensuring it cannot drip on to fresh food, and use different chopping boards for raw and cooked food.
● Cook food thoroughly and don't use food past its sell-by date.
● Keep pets out of the kitchen.
● Keep food covered.
● Never save uneaten food from the feeding bowl or undrunk milk from the bottle.
● Sterile bottles of breast milk or formula milk can be kept chilled in the refrigerator for up to 24 hours – after that they must be thrown away.

sterilizing

Whether feeding breast milk or formula milk, it is essential that all the equipment you use is thoroughly sterilized. Warm milk is the perfect feeding ground for bacteria. If teats and bottles are not washed thoroughly, your baby could become very ill. Most tummy upsets in babies are caused by poor hygiene when feeding.

There are three main methods of sterilizing: boil all the equipment for at least ten minutes in a large pan; soak the equipment in sterilizing solution for two hours and then rinse with boiling water; use an electric steam sterilizer. I found the steam sterilizer to be the easiest and most convenient method; just follow the instructions carefully.

As your baby is weaned onto solid food, it is best to sterilize his bowl and feeding spoons. However, as soon as he can crawl and put everything in reach into his mouth there is no need to continue sterilizing these items. Nevertheless, you should continue to sterilize any bottles you use for milk feeds up to the age of 1. With equipment that it is impractical to sterilize, such as saucepans and sieves, make sure you wash these items thoroughly in hot water and detergent, and rinse them well to remove any residues. There are two key things to remember:
● Sterile bottles of breast milk or formula milk can be kept chilled in the refrigerator for up to 24 hours. Follow manufacturer's guidelines for bottle insulators.
● Once your baby has finished feeding, get into the habit of rinsing and washing bottles ready for sterilizing. Always throw away any milk left over from a feed.

washing and drying equipment
Use an organic detergent, if possible, because they are much milder and far less likely to irritate if they come into contact with your baby's skin. If you have a dishwasher, make use of it, because the water goes to a much higher temperature and the crockery will be air dried. Let equipment air dry as much as possible and avoid drying with a tea-towel which may harbour germs, use kitchen paper instead.

essential equipment
● Bottles
● Teats
● Bottle cleaner
● Sterilizing equipment
● Expressor
● Bottle insulator
● Rubber ice-cube trays
● Ziplock freezer bags
● Airtight containers

● Steamer
● Nylon sieve
● Hand-held blender or electric food processor or blender
● Stainless-steel saucepan
● Plastic feeding bowl
● Shallow baby spoons
● Bibs

Ideally, you should aim to breastfeed for the first year of your baby's life, as breast milk is the perfect food for a baby. It's much easier to breastfeed if you establish a routine early on. Conversations with midwives, state-registered paediatric dieticians and breastfeeding counsellors, as well as my own experience and that of close friends, have convinced me that it is possible and beneficial to start getting into a routine soon after your baby is born. Achieving this may not be plain sailing, but the hard work will pay off when you suddenly find you can enjoy some quality time without having a screaming baby to cope with.

0-3 months

what's happening to
your baby

Your baby may be able to hold something at 3 months, but then again she may not be able to do so until she's 4 months old. Both are quite normal. Every child is different. These sections on your baby's development are meant as a guide; if you are concerned about any aspect of your baby's development, never be afraid to talk to your health visitor or family doctor.

your baby's weight and height

Your baby will undergo considerable change during these early months. One of the first things that you are likely to notice is her weight. It's normal for your baby to lose weight after birth before she regains it. This is especially common among breastfed babies. Formula-fed babies may not lose weight, or may lose only a little and quickly put it back on.

Once your baby has regained her birth weight, she will probably gain about 25g a day. To help you relax about her growth, your health visitor, midwife or doctor should give you a book containing growth charts, or something similar, which will enable you to plot your baby's weight and height over time. Whatever your baby's length at birth, she will gain about 2cm every month. But there will always be variations, such as twins, triplets and premature babies, as well as the child's position in the family (first child, second child, etc).

your baby's responses to the world

You will begin to notice how your baby responds to the outside world. Almost from the time she is born she will be startled by sudden, loud noises. In the first few weeks she will gradually start to focus on your face when it is close to her. By two weeks she will recognize both your face and voice. At around 1 month she may be able to lift her head briefly while lying on her stomach. An exciting milestone is when she smiles back at you, which can happen from around 6 weeks. At this stage, her eyes may be able to follow brightly coloured toys, and by the second month she may begin to make cooing noises and grasp an object if put in her hand.

your
routine

The traditional belief is that babies should be fed on demand. However, juggling family and work can leave you feeling exhausted and inadequate. For me, establishing a routine seemed a logical solution. I spoke to many midwives and health professionals and read extensively on the subject before creating a routine that made my life easier and, in turn, helped both my girls feel happy and secure. It was not always easy, but it was worth the effort, especially when, by 4 months, both were sleeping through the night. The books that I found most useful included "Birth to Five" by NHS and "The Contented Little Baby Book" by Gina Ford (Vermilion).

The routines I devised are relaxed and, in my experience, easily achievable by a busy modern mum. One of the main advantages of establishing a good routine is that you can quite quickly begin to understand your baby's needs. I was confident that if my girls had slept well and eaten well but were still crying, there was a reason for their stress or discomfort, which was often just that they needed to be held or changed. This knowledge helped me to feel more in control and calm, which in turn helped to make Ella and Jasmin relaxed babies. And remember that it is crucial that you do not forget to think about yourself. Sleep whenever you can during the day, eat healthy snacks in between meals, and drink lots of water.

weeks 1 and 2

your baby's first feeds

The first feed is very important and should be offered within the first hour of life outside the womb. This is when your baby is most alert and the instinct to suck is strong, and so is the ideal opportunity to commence breastfeeding. For the first few days your breasts produce a liquid called colostrum (see page 20). Feeding should be on demand for a normal weight, healthy-term baby. Hopefully, this will be little and often. However, many babies, naturally shocked by their birth, spend the first few days sleeping more than they will later on in order to recover. If your baby tends not to wake for feeds in the first few days, offer the breast every three or four hours to prevent long gaps. Waking her may seem a little unfair, but it will help to ensure an adequate milk supply on day three or four, and it will prevent your baby cramming lots of feeds into a short space of time. This will also help you to establish a routine. The length of feeds is individual and, as long as it is not painful to you, your baby should be left to suck. The feeding time can shorten when the milk comes in because greater volume is achieved with less effort; after time, it will gradually increase again.

your baby's feeds from 4 days old

After about four days your body stops producing colostrum and produces milk instead. By now your baby should be sucking on one breast for 15-20 minutes for each feed. It is important to remember which breast she drank from last so you can offer the other at the next feed. Each breast produces "fore" and "hind" milk. The fore milk is thirst-quenching and low in calories, but the hind milk is richer and more concentrated. By making sure each breast is emptied you will ensure she has drunk both types of milk. If your baby only drinks the fore milk she may be constantly hungry. As her appetite increases you will need to start offering her the second breast at each feed; if she's not lasting three hours between feeds she is probably ready for more milk. During the day, aim to feed approximately every three hours.

expressing milk

Even if you get into the habit of feeding your baby frequently this is rarely enough to ensure you make sufficient milk to meet her demands during growth spurts. So establish an expressing routine in the second or third week of feeding, once your milk has come in. This encourages your body to make more milk than your baby may need, but you will be producing enough milk for those times when her demand increases, preventing the need to feed more frequently, especially during the night. I know mums who have had to feed every two hours at night to help stimulate more milk during their baby's growth spurts. This is often when tiredness pushes mums to the limit and they either give up the routine or stop breastfeeding completely.

I found the best times of day for expressing were first thing in the morning, when sitting in bed, and at bedtime. An electric pump makes this easier. I then froze the milk for future use. If a breast is not empty after you have finished expressing, start the next feed on that breast. Express before or after her first and last feeds – approximately 50 to 75ml each time. During growth spurts, stop expressing and offer your baby the breast for longer.

your baby's sleep

Aim to have a regular getting-up time and bedtime for your baby, which will hopefully fit in with your daily routine. If she is not awake at around 7am, wake her up. Try to get her used to being settled at night by 11-ish. Let her have about four hours, continuous sleep at a time during the night, but no longer, as she needs frequent feeds to keep her energy levels up. For more advice speak to your 0egistered paediatrician. During the first two weeks try to aim for the following:

- After breakfast: approximately one-and-a-half-hours.
- After lunch: two to two-and-a-half hours, ideally between midday and 2-2.30pm.
- Mid-afternoon: one hour at around 3.30pm.
- Bedtime: around 7pm, but wake her up at 10-ish for a feed and then every four hours.

weeks 3 and 4

quantity of milk

The amount you should aim to feed your baby largely depends on her weight. Health authorities advise that a baby under 4 months of age will need to eat 150ml per kilogram of her body weight per day (e.g. a 3.5kg baby will need 525ml of milk a day). This is only a guide; hungrier babies may need an extra 25ml at some feeds. Larger feeds are best given early in the day or late at night. Avoid big feeds in the middle of the night so that your baby associates daytime with feeding and night-time with sleeping. This routine applies for breastfed and bottle-fed babies.

your baby's feeds

During the day, aim to feed approximately every three hours. You may notice by this stage that your baby needs to drink for at least 25 to 30 minutes on the first breast to empty it, and she may need more from the second as her appetite increases. Remember to begin the next feed with the second breast so she always gets all the hind milk.

expressing milk

In order to compensate for the extra demand for food during this growth spurt, you will need to reduce the amount you express by 25ml at the expressing times (before or after your first and last feeds).

your baby's sleep

- After breakfast: approximately one-and-a-half-hours.
- After lunch: two to two-and-a-half hours, ideally between midday and 2-2.30pm.
- Mid-afternoon: one hour at around 3.30pm.
- Bedtime: around 7pm, but wake her up at 10-ish for a feed and then every four hours.

weeks 5 to 8

your baby's weight gain

If your baby is gaining weight at a steady 150 to 200g a week, she is probably ready to move on to the next routine. If her weight gain is low, you may need to keep her on the same routine as weeks 3 and 4 until it improves. Speak to your health visitor, family doctor or registered paediatrician about any weight-gain concerns that you may have.

your baby's feeds

Start to leave slightly more time between the first three feeds of the day – up to three-and-a-half hours, but keep the 7pm and 10pm feeds as before. If your baby is not as interested in her breakfast feed as she used to be, she may still be full from her night-time feed, in which case you could start to reduce the amount of milk she drinks during the night. You can encourage her to accept this by offering cooled, boiled water before the breast at night feeds.

expressing milk

Before or after your first and last feeds – approximately 50 to 75ml each time – but it is a good idea to reduce the amount you express at 7am or stop expressing milk at this time completely.

your baby's sleep

As your baby gains weight and is taking most of her food during the day, she should be able to sleep for longer during the night.
- After breakfast: up to one hour.
- After lunch: two to two-and-a-half hours, ideally between midday and 2-2.30pm.
- Mid-afternoon: 45 minutes at around 3.30pm, if required.
- Bedtime: around 7pm, but wake her up at 10-ish for a feed.

week 9 to 4 months

Things are getting simpler by the day; all your effort in the first weeks is really starting to pay off.

your baby's feeds

At around 9 weeks babies often go through a growth spurt. Increase the feed for breastfed and bottle-fed babies at their early morning, mid-morning and suppertime feeds. Keep the first three feeds up to about three-and-a-half hours apart, but keep the 7pm and 10pm feeds as before.

expressing milk

Only express at the last feed.

your baby's sleep

With a routine, Ella and Jasmin started sleeping through the night at around 4 months. But they woke up, hungry, earlier than usual, so I gave them a small amount and finished off the feed at 7am. Before long they could last until breakfast again. As a guide, if your baby weighs about 5.5kg and is taking all of her daytime feeds, you can assume she's ready to sleep through the night. As a result, she'll need less sleep in the day (about three-and-a-half hours in total).
- After breakfast: about 45 minutes.
- After lunch: two hours (two-and-a-quarter hours maximum), ideally between midday and 2pm.
- Mid-afternoon: 30 minutes at about 3.30pm if required (by 4 months she should no longer need it).
- Bedtime: around 7pm, but wake her up at 10-ish for a feed.

colic

Advice differs, but many experts recommend one or more of the following tips.

● Make sure your baby is in a well-established routine, feeding well from each breast for the right amount of time and sleeping well during the day and night. Do not try to appease your baby by continually putting her to the breast, as she may just be taking in air and not milk.

● Breastfeeding mothers may try cutting out the following from their diet: drinks that contain caffeine (such as coffee, tea, cola), alcohol, onions, garlic and citrus fruits.

● Good things to include in your diet are: fennel tea or 1 tsp crushed dill seeds steeped in hot water – a friend of mine who is a midwife swears by this.

nocturnal babies

Babies do not know the difference between day and night. You need to teach them to associate daytime with feeding and social activities and night with longer periods of sleep. When you feed at night, try to do it in the dark without talking too much, to prevent overstimulating her.

awkward and painful breastfeeding

Take time to position the baby on the breast correctly. Poor positioning is often the main cause of sore or cracked nipples. Pain caused by incorrect positioning also affects the release of oxytocin, a hormone which sends a signal to the breast to release milk. It is therefore important that you are comfortable and at ease.

engorged breasts

Engorged breasts can be very painful. If your baby finds your breasts are too full to latch on to properly, you may need to express a little before a feed. Place warm, wet flannels on your breast and gently express a little by hand. If your breasts are really uncomfortable, put cabbage leaves in your bra in between feeds.

empty breasts

Gently squeeze your nipple between your thumb and forefinger to check if there is still any milk in your breast.

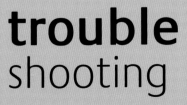

trouble
shooting

During the first six months of your baby's life, his birth weight is likely to double, and to sustain this growth he will eventually need more than just breast milk or formula milk. The weaning process, or the introduction of solid foods, begins at 4 to 6 months. At first, the food should be cooked to make it easier for your baby to eat and digest. First foods the world over are soft and bland, and usually mushy blends of staple foods that are easily digested, such as rice, non-citrus fruit or vegetables. Gradually, a more varied range of purées can be given to encourage your baby to chew and swallow and to broaden his appetite.

4-6 months

what's happening to
your baby

By 4 months, your baby is likely to be more settled and to have a routine. You will be able to tell whether he is happy or not and he will often indicate this by smiling and laughing out loud. He can recognize your smell and voice and increasingly will be able to focus on objects close to him, in particular, your face. When you put him on the floor, he may be able to roll over in one direction. At this stage he will also be staying awake for longer during the day and will be more alert. This is a great time to start playing simple games and having conversations. He is very likely to be amused by seeing his reflection in a mirror; try putting him in front of one and watch him chat away.

teething and sitting up

There is no fixed time for teething, but on average your baby's first teeth could appear at around 5 months. He may start to chew his hand or suck his thumb and even put his feet in his mouth – babies often chew and suck everything in sight! This can alleviate the pain of teething. He will begin to learn to sit and hold his head unsupported, and he will reach for things to hold and chew – these are good indications that he is ready to be weaned because he will have the coordination to pick up and move the spoon from bowl to mouth, although you will need to feed him at this stage. It is often during feeding when you discover that, as well as being able to coo with pleasure, your baby can squeal and scream with annoyance.

weaning

One of the easiest ways to judge whether a baby is ready to be weaned is by testing his tongue-thrust reflex. If you put a tiny amount of bland purée onto the end of your finger and gently put it onto the tip of your baby's tongue he will poke both the food and his tongue out almost immediately. This reflex clears any foreign bodies, including food, out of his mouth and so protects him from choking. At some point between 4 and 6 months this reflex disappears. Try a little experiment with your baby and see what his reaction is. If he sucks your finger instead of spitting out the food, it is a sure sign he is ready to try a little solid food.

At this stage, breast milk or infant formula milk is still providing all the nutrients that your baby needs. The introduction of other foods during weaning is simply to help your child become used to eating solids, and to learn how to swallow, rather than suck food off a spoon. As long as your baby is drinking milk as usual, there is no reason to be concerned about his nutritional intake. Remember to always wash all fruits and vegetables carefully before you cook them. And never leave a baby alone while feeding.

nutrition for immunity

Although your baby does not require solid food for nutritional reasons at this age, it is wise to give him foods that will help boost his immature immune system. This will aid his body's natural defence system, which fights off infections and diseases. The most important nutrients are:

Vitamin C – a powerful, immune-boosting vitamin that is great for helping to fight colds. It is also essential for assisting iron absorption. Carrots, mangoes, and broccoli are all good early weaning foods and great sources of vitamin C.

Vitamin E – an antioxidant vitamin vital for helping protect the body from diseases that occur later in life. Sweet potatoes and avocados are good sources and great early weaning foods.

Betacarotene – the body converts betacarotene into vitamin A, which is a good antioxidant.

Zinc – essential for a healthy immune system. Good sources for babies of this age include rice and green vegetables, such as peas and spinach.

which nutrients
are key

nutrients required per day

Milk provides a baby with all the nutrients he needs until he is 6 months old. I've assumed, per 100ml of milk, the lowest level of nutrients provided by the common brands on which the milk chart on page 21 is based. The quantity of milk (1000ml) and nutrients required (based on the Recommended Nutrient Intake) are based on a larger than average baby. If you're breastfeeding, your baby should get all nutrients he needs from you. *Although it seems babies need extra calcium from solids, because babies absorb nutrients more easily than adults this is not needed.

	protein 1 point = 1.5g	iron 1 point = 1.5mg	zinc 1 point = 1mg	calcium 1 point = 105mg	vitamin C 1 point = 5mg
total points recommended	8½ (12.7g)	3 (4.3mg)	4 (4mg)	5 (525mg)	5 (25mg)
milk (1000ml of formula) provides	9½ (14g)	3½ (5mg)	5 (5mg)	4½ (460g)	16½ (82mg)
points required from food	0	0	0	½ (*see caption)	0

the weaning
process

Weaning is a natural process in which you gradually introduce your baby to "solid" food. There are two main reasons for weaning; one is nutritional and the other is social.

Breast milk, or formula milk, is a complete food. It provides all the nutrients, energy, and liquid that your baby needs during his first few months. However, it is quite a dilute food, containing a high percentage of water. As your baby grows, breast milk alone will not satisfy him.

Solid foods are far more concentrated in terms of nutrients than breast milk, so tiny amounts will help to satisfy your baby. While a single solid food, such as puréed carrot, may be high in certain nutrients, it may be low in others, so it is important that your baby has a varied and balanced diet of solid foods to ensure healthy development.

The early stages of weaning are more about social change than nutrition. Breast of formula milk is still the main food. At this stage, babies are most receptive to new tastes. Babies given a large variety of non-allergy forming foods from the age of 4 months tend to accept a wider range of foods at 1 year than those weaned on a restricted diet. Children given lots of sweet things often prefer sweet foods through to at least the age of 2.

why wait to wean

Most babies are weaned when they are between 4 and 6 months old. Because every baby is unique, some may start later, but none should start earlier. Rushing things can be much more damaging for his health than continuing breast milk or formula milk feeds, because a baby's immature digestive system cannot cope with solid foods. Solid food can hinder a baby's ability to absorb nutrients, particularly iron, from breast milk or formula milk. There is growing evidence that giving solids too early increases the likelihood of your baby developing serious food allergies and intolerances.

when to wean

The most obvious sign that your baby is ready for weaning is that he will begin to last for less time between feeds and may be restless after them. He may be irritable and start to chew his hand or toys before the next feed is due, or he may begin to wake earlier than usual, especially at night. Other, less obvious, indications are:

- His tongue thrust reflex has diminished (see page 40).
- He may show an interest in the food you are eating, particularly by drooling – don't be tempted to give him your food.
- First teeth may develop.
- His weight may level off.
- He may be able to hold things.

Don't ignore these signs and leave weaning too late, as babies can be less receptive and less willing to try different flavours of food after 8 months or so.

how to wean a baby

Weaning requires patience and will entail a lot of mess, but it's a rewarding experience because your baby learns to eat with the family. A plastic sheet under the chair and a bib that catches food are useful. Try to feed your baby some solid food at family mealtimes. Even if you are by yourself, try to eat something at the same time – babies learn through example.

Baby rice diluted with breast milk or formula milk is the best food for the first week of weaning. I found lunchtime (late morning) to be the best time of day to introduce first food, as babies are alert and satisfied from their breakfast milk. All that is needed is 1–2 tsp baby rice or ground maize mixed with breast milk or formula milk.

As your baby becomes used to the new texture, you can begin to offer other foods, every three days or so, after his milk feed. Let your baby set the pace. Offer small tastes on the end of a plastic, shallow weaning spoon. (Never use a metal spoon – they can be sharp or too hot.) He may spit it out, but persevere. You can begin to introduce the second feed after his milk at suppertime, before bed. This will help to keep him satisfied until morning.

If any purée seems to be too thick, dilute it with breast milk or formula milk. During the first few weeks of weaning, the food ideally should be bland vegetable purées mixed with a little baby rice, breast milk or formula milk if they have strong flavours. Stick to single-ingredient purées for the first few weeks in order to identify any food to which your baby may have an adverse reaction.

Between the age of 5 and 6 months, you could introduce a third solid feed at around breakfast time, halfway through a milk feed. Purées now should be both non-citrus fruit and vegetable, but try to offer more vegetable purées than fruit. Ideally, by the end of the sixth month, your baby will be enjoying three small solid meals each day. If he is still not showing any real interest in solids you may need to reduce his milk intake slightly; however, he will still need 800-1000ml of milk each day.

Remember to take weaning slowly – it's better for the baby and better for you. Don't make any sudden changes. If you are breastfeeding and you wean your baby too quickly, your breasts will become extremely sore; they may get engorged and blocked and you could get mastitis.

foods to eat and
foods to avoid

It is important to wean your baby on as wide a range of foods as possible because he will learn to enjoy and appreciate food. However, you should introduce new foods gradually. Some foods can be dangerous for young babies, usually either because of the danger of food allergies or choking, and so these foods are not introduced until your baby is older. If there is any family history of allergies, you should always seek advice from your doctor or state-registered dietitian.

Foods to avoid at 4 to 6 months include:

- Foods containing gluten, such as wheat cereals and wheat flour, including bread and breakfast cereals, rye, barley, and oats.
- Eggs – the yolk and white are high in protein, which babies find hard to digest. They may also contain salmonella bacteria, which cause food poisoning.
- Citrus fruits, including juice, are too acidic. Their high sugar and fruit-acid content can contribute to tooth decay and may trigger an allergic reaction.
- Nuts and peanut butter can trigger a fatal nut allergy.
- Sugar is unnecessary; mix tart non-citrus fruit with sweeter non-citrus fruit to sweeten it.
- Honey can contain botulism spores that cause food poisoning.
- Salt can stress immature kidneys and cause dehydration.
- Dairy products can trigger allergic reactions. Soft cheeses may contain the food-poisoning bacteria listeria, which some babies are sensitive to.
- Fish and shellfish.
- Excessively hot or spicy foods that can burn or inflame a baby's stomach.
- Tea and coffee contain tannins, which inhibit iron absorption, and caffeine. Caffeine is a stimulant that babies cannot tolerate.

Foods to eat at 4 to 6 months include:

Give your baby a wide selection of non-citrus fruits and vegetables with his milk feeds. The best first fruits and vegetables are detailed in the vegetable and fruit purée recipes in this chapter (see pages 50-83). All fruits and vegetables should be washed and carefully peeled before being prepared. Always remove the core, pips, and any discoloured areas. Most should be cooked at this stage, bananas, avocados, and cucumbers are the exception. Make sure vegetables and fruits are ripe or they might be indigestible and need extra cooking, which will diminish their nutritional content.

   If any of your purées are too runny or too thick, add baby rice or breast milk or formula milk as appropriate to achieve a consistency that's easy for your baby to suck off the spoon. Similarly, you can use these ingredients to soften flavours that are too strong for your baby at this stage.

At 4-6 months, milk is still the most important source of nutrition – your baby should be getting all the nutrients he needs from his milk feeds. When you start to introduce solid foods, you need to continue to give your baby most of his milk feed first, then a little solid food, and then the remaining milk. This way you can ensure that your baby will drink as much milk as he needs and just a have a taste of the solid foods.

The "recommended daily volume of food" chart below is intended to be a guide. Obviously all babies have different needs, depending on many factors, including weight. You will have to follow your baby's direction and use your initiative when deciding how much to feed him each day. For example, if, after a week of weaning, you introduce a suppertime solid feed to your baby's routine only to find that he is too tired to eat it, you may need to try starting that feed a little bit earlier in the day.

recommended
daily intake

recommended daily volume of foods

milk = breastfeed or 200ml formula

	4 months old, week 1	4 months old, weeks 2-4	5 months old	6 months old
Breakfast, 7-8am	milk	milk	milk, then 1 portion breakfast	milk, then 1 portion breakfast
Lunch, 11.45-ish	milk alternated during feed with 1-2 tsp baby rice, increasing to 3-4 tsp	milk alternated during feed with 4-6 tsp fruit purée or vegetable purée	milk, then 1 portion vegetable purée	milk, then 1 portion vegetable purée
Mid-pm, 3pm	milk, cooled boiled water	milk, cooled boiled water	milk, cooled boiled water	milk, cooled boiled water
Supper, 6.30pm-ish	milk. In bed by 7pm-ish	milk, then 4-6 tsp baby rice mixed with fruit or vegetable purée. In bed by 7pm-ish	milk, then baby rice mixed with 1 portion vegetable or fruit purée or baby rice or a combination of the two, plus cooled boiled water. In bed by 7pm-ish	1 portion savoury and 1 portion fruit purée (the latter is optional), plus cooled boiled water or well-diluted fruit juice, then milk. In bed by 7pm-ish
Night time, 10pm	milk	milk	milk feed, but gradually reduce this as your baby's solids intake increases	milk feed, but gradually reduce this as your baby's solids intake increases
TOTAL MILK	breast milk or 800-1000ml formula, depending on baby size, inclusive of milk used in sauces, cereals	breast milk or 800-1000ml formula, depending on baby size, inclusive of milk used in sauces, cereals	breast milk or 800-1000ml formula, depending on baby size, inclusive of milk used in sauces, cereals	breast milk or 800-1000ml formula, depending on baby size, inclusive of milk used in sauces, cereals

your
routine

your baby's feeds

Continue to give most of the milk feed before offering solid food, then give a little solid food, then the remaining milk. Some experts recommend that in the early days you only introduce a new savoury or fruit or vegetable purée every two to three days to help prevent any problems with your baby's digestion – worth bearing in mind when you plan his menu (see page 48 and 49 for meal planners).

Ideally, at between 5 and 6 months old your baby will not need any milk after 7pm. To help achieve this, gradually reduce the amount of milk that you give him at 10pm and offer cooled, boiled water instead of milk. Babies soon realize that there is little point in waking up for water.

By 6 months, he should be eating three puréed meals a day. Try and focus on the lunchtime feed as the most important, and during this feed, try to alternate between milk and solids. Towards the end of month 6, gradually start to separate the solid feed from the milk feed at suppertime. Give him the solid feed at around 5pm with a drink of water and then the milk feed at bedtime.

your baby's sleeps

In an ideal world, your baby needs to sleep for approximately 45 minutes after breakfast and for two to two-and-a-quarter hours after lunch. I have suggested that you put your baby to sleep for a quick nap in the morning and then a longer sleep after lunch because this is what really worked for my girls and many of my friends' babies. But if it is impossible to fit this into your schedule, then change the routine to suit you. Do make sure, though, that your baby is awake by 3pm because this helps to ensure that he will be tired again by bedtime, at 7pm-ish.

frustration when eating

Some babies cry between spoonfuls of solid food, usually because they are frustrated. It may take them a little while to get used to the fact that solid-food feeding isn't continuous but interrupted, and that solids will satisfy their hunger.

messy eating

Don't worry if there is more purée over your kitchen than inside your baby. The weaning process in the early stages is more about getting him used to the food's taste and texture and the spoon than providing him with food. Milk will still satisfy all his nutritional needs. His lack of enthusiasm may be because he is not hungry; towards the end of the 6 months, try reducing the amount of milk feed you give before the solid food.

reluctance to eat

Never force your baby to eat solid food; it's unpleasant for him and he may choke. Eating is quite a difficult process for your baby to get the hang of because he is used to sucking. When you start feeding, use a flat spoon and let him suck the food off the end. Gradually he will learn to take the food and swallow without relying on the sucking reflex. Never try to force-feed by mixing solid food with milk in a bottle; this takes away his right to "say" no to solid food and to take weaning at his own pace. It can also make him choke.

a baby with a sweet tooth

Do not always give sweet food after savoury – it helps prevent your baby from believing that green vegetables are unpleasant and sweet foods a treat.

a stressed baby who won't eat

Sit him on your lap to reduce any stress he may feel.

breast to bottle-feeding

Don't switch from breast to bottle-feeding at the same time as weaning. Two major changes can be too much and make the baby confused, stressed, and less likely to adapt well during the transition stage.

trouble
shooting

sample meal planners

Always use the meal planner key (page 94)

One of the key things to remember when first weaning is to introduce new foods every three to four days. At the beginning it's also important to alternate solids with milk during a feed. Milk = breastfeed or 200ml formula.

4 months old, weeks 1-2

	breakfast	lunch	mid-afternoon	supper	10pm
days 1-7	milk	milk alternated at feed with 1-2 tsp baby rice, increasing to 3-4 tsp	milk and later water	milk	milk
days 8-11	milk	milk alternated at feed with 2-3 tsp carrot purée	milk and later water	milk, then 2-3 tsp baby rice with carrot purée, water	milk
days 12-14	milk	milk alternated at feed with 2-3 tsp pear purée	milk and later water	milk, then 2-3 tsp baby rice with pear purée, water	milk

4 months old, weeks 3-4

	breakfast	lunch	mid-afternoon	supper	10pm
day 1	milk	milk alternated at feed with 4-6 tsp squash and carrot purée, water	milk and later water	milk, then 4-6 tsp baby rice with 2-3 tsp apple purée, water	small milk
day 2	milk	milk alternated at feed with 4-6 tsp squash and carrot purée, water	milk and later water	milk, then 4-6 tsp baby rice with 2-3 tsp apple purée, water	small milk
day 3	milk	milk alternated at feed with 4-6 tsp squash and carrot purée, water	milk and later water	milk, then 4-6 tsp baby rice with banana purée, water	small milk
day 4	milk	milk, then 4-6 tsp pear purée, water	milk and later water	milk, 4-6 tsp baby rice with sweet potato and carrot purée, water	small milk
day 5	milk	milk, then 4-6 tsp pea and courgette purée, water	milk and later water	milk, then 4-6 tsp baby rice, water	small milk
day 6	milk	milk, then 4-6 tsp pea and courgette purée, water	milk and later water	milk, then 4-6 tsp baby rice with apple purée, water	small milk
day 7	milk	milk, then 4-6 tsp pear purée with baby rice, water	milk and later water	milk, then 4-6 tsp baby rice with apple purée, water	small milk

5 months old, any week

	breakfast	lunch	mid-afternoon	supper	10pm
day 1	milk, then mango purée, water	milk, then avocado purée with baby rice, water	milk and later water	milk, then a little baby rice, water	small milk
day 2	milk, then mango purée, water	milk, then avocado purée with baby rice, water	milk and later water	milk, then a little baby rice, water	small milk
day 3	milk, then baby rice, water	milk, then sweet potato purée, water	milk and later water	milk, then carrot purée, water	small milk
day 4	milk, then banana purée, water	milk, then broccoli purée, water	milk and later water	milk, then baby rice, water	small milk
day 5	milk, then banana purée, water	milk, then swede and carrot purée, water	milk and later water	milk, then baby rice, water	small milk
day 6	milk, then mango purée, baby rice, water	milk, then baby rice, water	milk and later water	milk, then apple and parsnip purée, water	small milk
day 7	milk, then apple and pear purée, water	milk, then parsnip purée, water	milk and later water	milk, then baby rice with pea purée, water	small milk

6 months old, any week

	breakfast	lunch	mid-afternoon	supper	10pm
day 1	milk, then apple and cinnamon purée	milk, pumpkin and leek purée, water	milk and later water	courgette purée, melon purée, water, then milk	small milk
day 2	milk, then apple and cinnamon purée	milk, then pumpkin and leek purée, water	milk and later water	courgette purée, melon purée, water, then milk	small milk
day 3	milk, then papaya and raspberry purée	milk, then pumpkin and leek purée, water	milk and later water	broccoli purée, apricot purée, water, then milk	small milk
day 4	milk, then papaya and raspberry purée	milk, then carrot purée, water	milk and later water	swede and carrot purée, apple purée, water, milk	small milk
day 5	milk, then mango and peach purée	milk, then parsnip and potato purée, water	milk and later water	swede and carrot purée, apple purée, water, then milk	small milk
day 6	milk, then mango and peach purée	milk, then parsnip and potato purée, water	milk and later water	beetroot and carrot purée, water, milk	small milk
day 7	milk, then apricot and banana purée	milk, then parsnip and potato purée, water	milk and later water	beetroot and carrot, water, then milk	small milk

fresh breakfasts

blueberry and pear purée

makes: 3 baby portions or 1 baby portion and 1 adult portion as a smoothie base

storage: up to 24 hours in the refrigerator

1 ripe pear, eg Williams
4–5 tbsp water
large handful of fresh
  blueberries

Keep an eye out for the wild version of blueberries, known as bilberries. They are available in late summer and are very distinctive because they have a really bright blue juice. For a smoothie, add apple juice to taste.

1 Peel and core the pear and cut into bite-size chunks.
2 Put into a saucepan with the water and the blueberries.
3 Simmer for a few minutes until the pear is tender and the blueberries just burst.
4 Whiz with a hand-held blender (or in a food processor or blender) until smooth. Leave to cool before serving.
5 For just-weaned babies, sieve the purée using a nylon sieve.

papaya and raspberry purée

makes: 3 baby portions or 1 baby portion and 1 adult portion as a smoothie base

storage: up to 24 hours in the refrigerator

1 ripe papaya
handful of fresh raspberries

Most fruits for babies at this age need to be cooked. A really ripe papaya should have a wonderful scent of the fruit and should just give when gently squeezed. For a smoothie, add orange juice to taste.

1 Cut the papaya in half and scoop out the seeds. Peel each half and cut the flesh into cubes.
2 Put the papaya and raspberries in a pan with 2 tbsp water and simmer for a few minutes, or until the raspberries have burst.
3 Whiz the papaya with the raspberries using a hand-held blender (or in a food processor or blender) until smooth.
4 For just-weaned babies, sieve the purée using a nylon sieve.

Before feeding your baby any of these purées, please read the section on weaning (pages 42/43) and the 4-6 month sample meal planners (pages 48/49)

melon mania purée

makes: 4 baby portions or 1 baby portion and 2 adult portions as a smoothie base

storage: up to 24 hours in the refrigerator

200g piece cantaloupe melon
200g piece galia melon
baby rice or mashed ripe banana, to thicken

Melons have a high water content, so they don't need cooking and are easily digested. This is a particularly lovely purée to serve on a hot day because it is naturally cooling. If the purée is a little too thin, add some mashed banana or baby rice, which will also help offset the melon's sweetness. For a smoothie, add a little lime juice. Alternatively, just make half the recipe, which is sufficient for two baby portions. Note that melon is mildly laxative.

1 Scoop out the seeds from each piece of melon and then spoon out the flesh of the fruit – use only the flesh that can easily be scooped out. If you find you have to scrape hard to get the flesh away from the edges, it will not be ripe enough for your baby to eat.

2 Steam or simmer the melon with 2 tbsp water for a few minutes, until soft.

3 Whiz the melon with a hand-held blender (or in a food processor or blender) until smooth. Add enough baby rice or mashed banana to thicken to a purée consistency before serving.

mango and peach purée

makes: 3 baby portions or 1 baby portion and 1 adult portion as a smoothie base

storage: up to 24 hours in the refrigerator

1 small, ripe mango
1 small, ripe peach

Mango is one of many tropical fruits that are naturally sweet and don't need cooking. However, it can also be quite intensely flavoured, so at first you may wish to dilute it with a little baby rice. Some mangoes can be a bit fibrous, so it is best to pass a purée of a particularly stringy mango through a nylon sieve.

1 Slice through the mango on either side of the stone. Peel, then cut the flesh into cubes.

2 Put the peach in a small bowl and pour over boiling water. Leave for 2 minutes. Drain and rinse with cold water. Peel the skin off the peach, remove the stone and cut the flesh into chunks.

3 Steam or simmer the peach and mango with 3 tbsp water for a few minutes, until soft.

4 Whiz the mango and peach with a hand-held blender (or in a food processor or blender) until smooth.

apricot and banana purée

makes: 3 baby portions or 1 baby portion and 1 adult portion as a smoothie base

storage: up to 24 hours in the refrigerator

3 ripe fresh apricots
1 small ripe banana

Choose bananas that are fully ripe – that means ones with small black spots. Just make sure they are not split or bruised. Bananas often have high levels of pesticide residues, so if you can buy organic bananas this is advisable. They are now widely available, and many supermarkets also sell the smaller varieties which means less waste! Apricots have an intense fresh taste that babies love – choose fruits that feel heavy for their size and have a strong apricot scent.

1 Remove the stones from the apricots. Peel them and cut the flesh into small pieces. Put into a saucepan with 4 tbsp water.
2 Heat gently for about 4-5 minutes, until the apricots are soft and pulpy. Cool the fruit.
3 Peel the banana. Whiz the apricots and banana together with a hand-held blender (or in a food processor or blender) until smooth.
4 For just-weaned babies, pass the purée through a nylon sieve.

peach and raspberry purée

makes: 2 baby portions or 1 baby portion plus 1 small adult portion as a smoothie base

storage: up to 24 hours in the refrigerator

1 small ripe peach
handful of fresh raspberries

Just like adults, babies appreciate food that is interesting to look at as well as tasting good. This purée is a fabulous vibrant pink – great for encouraging a less-than-keen baby to try some solid food!

1 Put the peach in a small bowl and pour over boiling water. Leave for 2 minutes. Drain and rinse with cold water. Peel the skin off the peach, remove the stone and cut the flesh into chunks.
2 Put the raspberries and peach into a pan with 2-3 tbsp water and heat gently for a few minutes, until soft. Cool.
3 Whiz together the raspberries and peach with a hand-held blender (or in a food processor or blender) until smooth.
4 For just-weaned babies, pass the purée through a nylon sieve.

quick bites **breakfasts**

At first, weaning is not about giving your baby nutrients through solid foods, but rather it is about introducing new textures and tastes and encouraging your baby to have an interest in food. All these quick ideas use ingredients that take very little time to prepare or cook.

things to purée with banana

Take ½ ripe banana (look for little brown spots on the banana's skin to make sure it is really ripe), peel, and cut the flesh into small pieces.

blueberries

handful of ripe blueberries
½ ripe banana, cut into small pieces

Put the blueberries in a saucepan with 1 tbsp water and cook for 2-3 minutes, until the fruit just starts to burst open. Transfer to a bowl, add the chopped banana and whiz with a hand-held blender (or in a food processor or blender) until smooth. For just weaned babies, push through a nylon sieve.

peach

½ ripe peach
½ ripe banana, cut into small pieces

Peel and chop the peach and put it into a small pan. Add 2 tbsp water and cook for 5 minutes, until the flesh is just soft. Add the chopped banana and whiz together with a hand-held blender (or in a food processor or blender) until smooth.

papaya

½ ripe papaya
½ ripe banana, cut into small pieces

Peel and chop the flesh of the papaya and put it into a small pan. Add 2 tbsp water and cook for 3-4 minutes. Add the chopped banana and whiz with a hand-held blender (or in a food processor or blender) until smooth or mash.

pear

1 ripe pear
½ ripe banana, cut into small pieces

Peel and core the pear and cut the flesh into pieces. Put the pieces into a small pan. Add 2 tbsp water and cook for 5 minutes. Add the chopped banana and whiz together with a hand-held blender (or in a food processor or blender) until smooth.

things to purée with baby rice

Make up 2 tbsp baby rice following the instructions on the packet, using breast or formula milk or cooled boiled water.

2 ½ ½

½ ripe mango
2 tbsp baby rice made as above

mango

Peel the mango and cut the flesh into small pieces. Put into a pan with 2 tbsp water and cook for a few minutes, until just soft. Add the baby rice and whiz with a hand-held blender (or in a food processor or blender) until smooth.

2 ½

1 ripe pear
2 tbsp baby rice made as above

pear

Peel and core half a pear. Cut the flesh into small pieces. Put into a pan with 2 tbsp water and simmer gently for 5 minutes, or until soft. Add the baby rice and whiz with a hand-held blender (or in a food processor or blender) until smooth.

1

½ ripe banana
2 tbsp baby rice made as above

banana

Peel the banana and chop the flesh into small pieces. Add the baby rice and whiz with a hand-held blender (or in a food processor or blender) until smooth.

½

1 eating apple
2 tbsp baby rice made as above

apple

Peel and core the apple, then cut into small pieces and put into saucepan with 2 tbsp water. Simmer gently for 5 minutes, or until soft. Add the baby rice and whiz with a hand-held blender (or in a food processor or blender) until smooth.

really quick things to cook with apple purée

Take 1 eating apple, eg Cox's orange pippin. Peel, core, and cut into small pieces.

½

1 small carrot
1 eating apple, chopped as above

carrot

Peel the carrot, then cut it into small pieces. Put it into a saucepan with the apple pieces and a little water and cook until just tender – approximately 3-5 minutes. Drain off a little water and then whiz with a hand-held blender (or in a food processor or blender) until smooth.

½ ½

1 small parsnip
1 eating apple, chopped as above

All quick bites make 1 portion unless otherwise stated.

parsnip

Peel the parsnip, then cut it into 1.5cm pieces. Put into a saucepan with a little water and cook for 5–10 minutes. Add the apple pieces and continue to cook for a few minutes until the apple is just tender. Drain off a little water and whiz with a hand-held blender (or food processor or blender) until smooth. For just-weaned babies, sieve the purée using a nylon sieve.

breakfasts **to freeze**

cherry and apple purée

makes: 3 baby portions

storage: up to 2 months in the freezer

handful of fresh cherries
3 eating apples, eg Cox's
  orange pippin

Make this purée in early summer, when there is a glut of cherries and they are not too expensive. The larger, darker cherries tend to be sweeter. If you have the time or are doing this in bulk, it may be easier to stone the cherries before you cook them – do this over a clean bowl so that you can catch all the juice. Cherry stoners are available in most kitchen shops.

1 Remove any stalks or leaves from the cherries.
2 Peel and core the apples and cut into chunks. Put into a pan with 4 tbsp water. Add the cherries and heat gently until the apples are soft and pulpy and the cherries are releasing their juice. Allow to cool.
3 Push the fruit through a nylon sieve, or purée using a mouli.
4 Spoon the purée into ice-cube trays. Cover with foil or put into a freezer bag and seal. Freeze.
5 Thaw thoroughly to serve.

plum and pear purée

makes: 3 baby portions

storage: up to 2 months in the freezer

3 ripe plums, eg Victoria
  plums or greengages
2 ripe pears, eg Williams

Before feeding your baby any of these purées, please read the section on weaning (pages 42/43) and the 4-6 month sample meal planners (pages 48/49)

This is a great autumnal purée. Try different varieties of plums to see which your baby likes. Victoria plums have a mild flavour; greengages can be sharper if they are not fully ripe, so make sure you choose sweet-smelling and slightly soft fruits. Swirl a little through some yogurt for a quick breakfast for yourself.

1 Remove the stalks from the plums. Halve the fruit, remove the stones. Peel, and cut the flesh into chunks.
2 Peel and core the pears and cut into chunks.
3 Put both the fruits into a pan with 3 tbsp water and heat gently until the fruit is soft and pulpy. Whiz with a hand-held blender (or in a food processor or blender) until smooth. For just-weaned babies, push through a nylon sieve.
4 Spoon the purée into ice-cube trays. Cover with foil or put into a freezer bag and seal. Freeze.
5 Thaw thoroughly to serve.

raspberry and pear purée

makes: 2 baby portions or 1 baby portion and 1 small adult portion as a smoothie base

storage: up to 2 months in the freezer

1 ripe pear e.g. Williams
50g or large handful of fresh raspberries
4-5 tbsp water

The colour of this purée is particularly appealing. To make a smoothie, just add apple juice to taste.

1 Peel and core the pear and cut it into bite-sized chunks.
2 Put the pear into a saucepan with the raspberries and water. Simmer for a few minutes until the pear is tender and the raspberries have just burst open – it won't take long.
3 Whiz with a hand-held blender (or in a food processor or blender) until smooth, then leave to cool before serving.
4 For just-weaned babies, sieve the purée, using a nylon sieve.
5 Spoon the purée into ice-cube trays. Cover with foil or put into a freezer bag and seal. Freeze.
6 To serve, thaw thoroughly.

apple and cinnamon purée

makes: 2 baby portions

storage: up to 2 months in the freezer

4 eating apples, eg Cox's orange pippin
10 tbsp water
¼ tsp ground cinnamon

This is a great purée to make in the autumn, when there is a glut of apples. Look for locally grown apples and do a bit of experimenting with different varieties – many British eating apples cook just as well as cookers and have a much fruitier taste. As with all weaning foods, resist the temptation to sweeten the purée with sugar if you feel it is a little tart. Try feeding first; if it's not successful, sweeten with another fruit such as bananas. A little spice, such as cinnamon, can be introduced once your baby has been taking solids for at least a month.

1 Peel and core the apples. Slice.
2 Put the apples into a saucepan with the water and cinnamon.
3 Heat gently for 15-20 minutes, until the apples are soft and pulpy, mashing occasionally with a wooden spoon. Cool.
4 Whiz with a hand-held blender (or in a food processor or blender) until smooth.
5 Spoon the purée into ice-cube trays. Cover with foil or put into a freezer bag and seal. Freeze.
6 To serve, thaw thoroughly.

apple and pear purée

½

2 **C**

makes: 2 baby portions

storage: up to 2 months in the freezer

2 eating apples, such as
   Cox's orange pippin
2 pears
½ tsp cinnamon

This is a great purée to make in the autumn, when there are lots of apples and pears. You could always make a larger quantity and add a good dollop to your breakfast cereal or yogurt. A little spice, such as cinnamon, can be introduced once your baby has been taking solids for at least a month.

1 Peel and core the apples and pears and slice.
2 Put into a saucepan with 10 tbsp water and the cinnamon.
3 Heat gently until the fruit is soft and pulpy, mashing occasionally with a wooden spoon; this will take about 15-20 minutes. Allow to cool.
4 Whiz with a hand-held blender (or in a food-processor or blender until smooth. Spoon the purée into ice-cube trays, cover with foil or put into a freezer bag and seal. Freeze.
5 Thaw thoroughly to serve.

apricot and mango purée

1

makes: 3 baby portions

storage: up to 2 months in the freezer

4 dried apricots
1 small ripe mango

Most dried apricots are treated with sulphur dioxide, a preservative that can cause an allergic reaction. Organic apricots are untreated and tend to be harder and darker in colour but, if anything, have a more intense and apricot-y flavour. This is another beautifully coloured purée – and the little frozen cubes make great summer treats for toddlers.

1 Put the apricots in a small bowl and pour over 4 tbsp boiling water. Leave to soak until they are soft and plump (about half an hour).
2 Slice through the mango either side of the stone. Peel, then cut the flesh into cubes.
3 Drain the apricots, reserving the soaking liquid, and finely chop them.
4 Put the mango, chopped apricots, and apricot-soaking liquid into a pan. Cook gently until the mango has broken down and the apricot pieces are soft (about 5–10 minutes). You may need to add 2-3 tbsp water if the fruit becomes too dry. Cool.
5 Whiz the fruits together with a hand-held blender (or in a food processor or blender) until smooth.
6 For a just-weaned baby, pass the purée through a nylon sieve.
7 Spoon the purée into ice-cube trays. Cover with foil or put into a freezer bag and seal. Freeze.
8 Thaw thoroughly to serve.

fresh savouries

avocado and cucumber purée

½

2 **C**

makes: 2 baby portions

storage: eat immediately

¼ **small cucumber**

½ **ripe avocado**

This is a simple, no-cook purée with a texture that most babies love. To make the most of the avocado, slice the remaining half and add it to a salad or sandwich for your lunch. Avocados contain healthy unsaturated fats that are essential to help keep your energy levels up when you are breastfeeding. They are also good for your skin.

1 Peel the cucumber and slice in half lengthways. Scrape out the seeds with a teaspoon. Chop into small chunks.
2 Peel, stone, and chop the avocado.
3 Whiz the cucumber and avocado with a hand-held blender (or in a food processor) until smooth. For just-weaned babies, push through a nylon sieve.

pea, mint and potato purée

1½

½

½

1 **C**

Vitamin B₁

makes: 3 baby portions

storage: up to 24 hours in the refrigerator

1 **small floury potato,**
  eg King Edward

100g **peas, fresh or frozen**

1 **fresh mint leaf**

Adding a small amount of fresh herbs or seasonings is a great way to stimulate your baby's appetite and to broaden his palate. Mint and peas have a natural affinity with each other, and using potatoes as the base is a good way to introduce new vegetables gradually into your baby's diet.

1 Peel the potato and cut into small dice. Bring a small pan of water to the boil, add the potatoes and cook until tender (approximately 10-12 minutes).
2 A couple of minutes before they are cooked, add the peas. Continue to simmer until just tender.
3 Drain, add the mint, and allow to cool slightly before whizzing with a hand-held blender (or in a food processor or blender) until smooth.
4 For just-weaned babies, pass the purée through a nylon sieve.

Before feeding your baby any of these purées, please read the section on weaning (pages 42/43) and the 4-6 month sample meal planners (pages 48/49)

sweet potato and onion purée

Vitamin A

makes: 5 baby portions or 1 baby portion and 2 adult portions as the base for a soup

storage: up to 24 hours in the refrigerator

1 small mild onion, peeled and finely chopped
1 medium sweet potato, peeled and finely chopped

Look for white sweet potatoes, which actually have deep yellow flesh, rather than the big red sweet potatoes (also known as yams). The white ones are less rich and have a fluffier texture when cooked, which babies seem to love. You can substitute them for ordinary potatoes in almost any recipe. A little pinch of ginger will accentuate their flavour and make the purée more interesting for your baby.

1 Put the onion and potato in a saucepan and just cover the vegetables with water.
2 Bring to the boil and simmer gently until the potato is soft (approximately 15 minutes). Drain and cool.
3 Whiz with a hand-held blender (or in a food processor or blender) until the purée is smooth.
4 For just-weaned babies, push through a nylon sieve.

potato and sweetcorn purée

makes: 2 baby portions

storage: best eaten immediately or stored for up to 24 hours in the refrigerator

1 medium floury potato, eg King Edward
1 cob fresh sweetcorn or 85g frozen sweetcorn

This is another great combination – potato is the most fantastic base for almost any vegetable purée, and it's particularly good for just-weaned babies. Look for organic sweetcorn, which is now available frozen. Non-organic sweetcorn is one of the most commonly genetically modified foods and is often specifically modified to make it sweeter, which means it loses its delicious nuttiness. A little chopped parsley or chives would be a great addition to this purée.

1 Peel the potato and cut into small chunks.
2 Remove the outer leaves of the sweetcorn and any stringy bits clinging to the cob. Using a sharp knife, cut the kernels away from the cob, turning it around as you go.
3 Bring a pan of water to the boil and add the potato and corn. Bring to the boil and simmer for about 6 minutes, or until the vegetables are tender. Drain and cool.
4 Whiz with a hand-held blender (or in a food processor or blender) until smooth. Add breast or formula milk to achieve desired consistency.
5 For just-weaned babies, pass the purée through a nylon sieve.

avocado and pea purée

1½

½

½

½

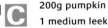
Vitamin B₁

makes: 2 baby portions

storage: best eaten
immediately or within 2 hours

60g peas, fresh or frozen
1 ripe medium avocado

Another beautifully coloured purée, provided you don't leave it hanging around too long because avocado does have a tendency to discolour. Ripe avocado has a lovely rich and creamy texture, which babies love. For babies used to herbs, add a couple of fresh coriander leaves to the purée to give it a little zing. If there is any of this purée left over, spread it on toast and top with Parma ham for a quick snack for you.

1 Bring a pan of water to the boil, add the peas, and then bring back to the boil and cook until just tender (approximately 3-4 minutes). Drain and leave to cool.
2 Peel, stone, and chop the avocado.
3 Whiz the peas and avocado together with a hand-held blender (or in a food processor or blender) until smooth.
4 For just-weaned babies, pass the purée through a nylon sieve.

pumpkin and leek purée

½

½

1

Vitamin A

makes: 3 baby portions

storage: up to 24 hours in the refrigerator

200g pumpkin flesh
1 medium leek

Pumpkin and squash tend to be rather neglected as a baby food, but their creamy texture and sweet nuttiness are always popular with babies. When I lived in South America for a couple of years during my childhood, my mother frequently cooked pumpkin and squash in many inspirational ways. This purée is best given once the baby has eaten a few other purées and is used to different flavours, because the leek can be quite strong. You may prefer to use slightly less leek.

1 Scrape away the seeds and stringy flesh from the pumpkin, and peel off the skin. Chop into small chunks.
2 Remove any tough outer leaves from the leek and trim the ends of the vegetable. Slice lengthways and clean under running water to remove any grit. Cut into 1.5cm chunks.
3 Put the vegetables into a steamer or colander over a pan of boiling water.
4 Cover with a lid and steam for 8 minutes, until they are tender.
5 Allow to cool slightly before whizzing with a hand-held blender (or in a food processor or blender) until smooth. For just-weaned babies, push through a nylon sieve. Leave to cool a little more before serving.

broccoli and potato purée

makes: 3 baby portions

storage: up to 24 hours in the refrigerator

2
½

½

3

1 medium head of broccoli
1 small floury potato,
   eg King Edward

Introduce the darker green vegetables as early as possible and your baby will be less likely to develop an aversion to them later on. Mixing them with potato should make them more palatable to begin with.

1 Remove all the tough stalks from the broccoli. Cut into small florets.
2 Peel the potato and cut it into small dice.
3 Put the vegetables into a steamer or colander over a pan of boiling water. Cover with a lid and steam for 10 minutes until they are tender.
4 Allow to cool slightly before whizzing with a hand-held blender (or in a food processor or blender) until smooth. Leave to cool a little more before serving. You might like to add a few drops of breast milk or formula milk if your purée is too thick.

beetroot and potato purée

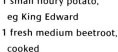

makes: 3 baby portions

storage: up to 24 hours in the refrigerator

1
½

½

½

1 small floury potato,
   eg King Edward
1 fresh medium beetroot,
   cooked

This is a beautiful ruby-red colour, with quite a sweet subtle flavour. You could use ready-cooked, vacuum-packed beetroot, but make sure it has not been doused in vinegar.

1 Peel the potato and cut into dice. Bring a pan of water to the boil, add the potato, and cook until tender (approximately 7 minutes). Drain.
2 Peel the beetroot, wearing clean rubber gloves if you do not want the shock of bright-pink-stained hands. Chop the flesh into small pieces. Add to the potato. Whiz with a hand-held blender (or in a food processor or blender) until smooth.

courgette and cauliflower purée

makes: 3 baby portions

storage: up to 24 hours in the refrigerator

1 courgette
50g cauliflower
1 medium potato

Cauliflower and courgettes are best steamed because the nutrients they contain are easily destroyed by overcooking. Steaming also means that fewer nutrients will be lost in the cooking water. Adding a few of the cauliflower's tender green inner leaves will increase the purée's vitamin C content. At the early weaning stage, it may be best to increase the ratio of courgette to cauliflower to reduce the chances of your baby becoming windy.

1 Remove the ends of the courgette and cut into chunks.
2 Cut the cauliflower into small florets. Peel the potato and cut into small pieces.
3 Put the vegetables into a steamer or colander over a pan of boiling water.
4 Cover with a lid and steam for 8 minutes, until tender. Cool before whizzing with a hand-held blender (or in a food processor or blender) until smooth.

squash and carrot purée

makes: 5 baby portions or 3 baby portions and 1 adult portion as the base for a soup

storage: best eaten immediately or stored for up to 24 hours in the refrigerator

½ large butternut squash
2 medium carrots

Vitamin A

Baby carrots may taste delicious, but they are far less nutritionally beneficial than the deeper-orange, older carrots – which are also much less expensive! Organic carrots often have a better flavour as well as being better for your baby, so look out for them. Even better, join a box delivery scheme where you can make the most of freshly picked, seasonal produce.

1 Cut the squash in half and scoop out the seeds. Peel and cut into small chunks.
2 Peel the carrots and cut into chunks.
3 Put the vegetables into a steamer or colander over a pan of boiling water
4 Cover with a lid and steam for 10-15 minutes, until just tender. Cool before whizzing with a hand-held blender (or in a food processor or blender) until smooth.

quick bites veggie purées

Some parents like to start their baby off on single-food purées. This is a great way to introduce your baby to a variety of tastes. You may need to add breast milk or formula milk or a baby rice to these purées to make the desired consistency.

asparagus

makes 2 portions
4 fresh asparagus stalks

Asparagus is great for the immune system and is a good source of betacarotene, essential for healthy skin and lungs. It also contains vitamin C, potassium, folic acid and riboflavin. Use fresh asparagus (look for stalks with clean, pale-green ends) and choose medium-size stalks. Asparagus is best eaten on the day it is bought. Snap off tough ends of the stalks. Cut each stalk into 4 pieces and steam for 5-10 minutes, then whiz with a hand-held blender (or in a food processor or blender) until smooth, with no stringy bits.

beetroot

1 raw, firm, medium beetroot

Beetroot is a good source of vitamins and minerals, especially vitamins B_6 and C, beta-carotene, potassium, calcium, iron, and folic acid. It is a great immune-boosting food. Cut off the stalk ends of the beetroot. Boil for 25-30 minutes, until tender. Drain and leave to cool, then peel. Whiz the flesh with a hand-held blender (or in a food processor or blender) until smooth.

avocado

1 ripe avocado

Avocados are rich in monounsaturated fats, which promote healthy skin. They are also easily digested, making them great for babies. Avocados can be served raw; pick a ripe one that gives slightly when pressed around the neck. Cut the avocado in half, twist to separate. Scrape the flesh from one half into a bowl. Mash with a fork or a blender to make a purée. Make this just before serving.

peas

handful of frozen peas

Peas are rich in vitamin C, the B vitamins, and iron. Put the peas in a pan of boiling water, bring back to the boil and cook for 1 minute. Whiz with a hand-held blender until smooth or, for just-weaned babies, push through a sieve. Fresh peas should be cooked for longer, puréed and sieved for babies up to 6 months.

3 C 1

makes 2 portions
1 medium broccoli head

broccoli

Broccoli is an excellent source of iron, particularly because it is a good source of vitamin C, essential in aiding the absorption of iron. It is also an immune-boosting food. Cut off the hard stalk from the broccoli head. Remove a quarter of the florets and steam them for 5-10 minutes until tender. Whiz with a hand-held blender (or in a food processor or blender) until smooth.

   ½ C 1 ½

florets and tender leaves of ¼ small
cauliflower

cauliflower

Cauliflower has high levels of vitamin C and folic acid. Try adding some tender green inner leaves to the purée, as this will increase its vitamin C content. Put the cauliflower florets and tender leaves into a steamer and steam for 10 minutes, or boil for 8 minutes, until tender. Whiz with a hand-held blender (or in a food processor or blender) until smooth.

   ½ C 1 ½

Vitamin A

1 medium carrot

carrot

Carrots are an excellent first food for babies because they rarely trigger an allergic reaction. Smaller carrots may be sweeter, but older darker carrots have a higher nutrient content. Carrots are also a good treatment for diarrhoea. If you buy organic carrots there is no need to peel them; just scrub them well. Non-organic carrots will need to be peeled. Chop your carrot into small pieces and boil or steam until tender (approximately 5 minutes). Whiz with a hand-held blender (or in a food processor or blender) until smooth.

   ½ C 1 ½

1 medium parsnip

parsnip

Parsnips are a good source of minerals and vitamins. They also help to relieve constipation. Top and tail the parsnip and peel and cut it into small pieces, then steam over boiling water for 6-8 minutes, until tender. Whiz with a hand-held blender (or in a food processor or blender) until smooth.

 3½ C ½ ½

Vitamin A, B₁

2 small courgettes

courgette

Courgettes are rich in vitamin C, folic acid, and potassium. Choose small, young courgettes, which will not need to be peeled, as they have tender, soft skins. It is better to choose organic, as any pesticide residues would be found in the skin. Remove the ends from the courgettes and slice into small rounds. Steam or boil until tender (10-15 minutes). Whiz with a hand-held blender (or in a food processor or blender) until smooth, with no stringy bits.

All quick bites make 1 portion,
unless otherwise stated.

savouries to freeze

sweetcorn and squash purée

makes: 5 baby portions

storage: up to 2 months in the freezer

½ **small butternut squash**
1 **fresh cob sweetcorn**

Try to choose organic fresh sweetcorn to make sure that it has not been genetically modified. If you cannot find fresh corn on the cob, use frozen sweetcorn because this is normally picked and frozen while still very fresh.

1 Cut the squash in half, scoop out the seeds, and remove the peel. Cut the flesh into small chunks.
2 Remove the leaves from the sweetcorn and any stringy bits clinging to it. Using a sharp knife, cut the kernels away from the cob, turning it around as you go.
3 Bring a pan of water to the boil and add the squash and corn (if using frozen corn, add later). Return to the boil, then simmer until the vegetables are tender. Drain and cool.
4 Whiz with a hand-held blender (or in a food processor or blender) until smooth.
5 For just-weaned babies, pass the purée through a nylon sieve. Spoon the purée into ice-cube trays. Cover with foil or put into a freezer bag and seal. Freeze.
6 To serve, thaw thoroughly and then reheat.

beetroot and carrot purée

Vitamin A

makes: 3 baby portions

storage: up to 2 months in the freezer

1 **fresh medium beetroot**
2 **small carrots**

Before feeding your baby any of these purées, please read the section on weaning (pages 42/43) and the 4-6 month sample meal planners (pages 48/49)

If you cannot find whole, fresh beetroot, use cooked beetroot – but do make sure that it has not been pickled in vinegar. Beetroot does have quite an intense flavour, so you may like to mix this purée with a little baby rice when you first introduce it.

1 Cut the top off the beetroot's stem. Bring a pan of water to the boil and add the beetroot. Cook until tender (about 30 minutes). Drain and leave to cool. Slip the skin off (wearing clean rubber gloves) and cut the flesh into small dice.
2 Peel the carrot and cut into dice. Bring a pan of water to the boil, add the carrot and cook until tender (approximately 3-4 minutes).
3 Drain and add to the beetroot. Whiz with a hand-held blender (or in a food processor or blender) until smooth. For just-weaned babies, pass the purée through a nylon sieve. Spoon into ice-cube trays, cover with foil and seal. Freeze.
4 To serve, thaw thoroughly and then reheat.

sweet potato and carrot purée

makes: 5 baby portions

storage: up to 2 months in the freezer

2 medium carrots
1 small sweet potato

Vitamin A

Adding a little chopped fresh coriander to this purée will give it a bit of zing, and the herb goes really well with the carrots. Both sweet potatoes and carrots are excellent sources of betacarotene, an antioxidant that helps to fight disease.

1 Peel and chop the carrots. Peel the sweet potato and cut into small chunks.
2 Put the vegetables into a steamer or colander over a pan of boiling water.
3 Cover with a lid and steam for 8 minutes, until the vegetables are tender. Cool before whizzing with a hand-held blender (or in a food processor or blender) until smooth.
4 Spoon the purée into ice-cube trays. Cover with foil or put into a freezer bag and seal. Freeze.
5 To serve, thaw thoroughly and then reheat.

root vegetable medley

makes: 5 baby portions

storage: up to 2 months in the freezer

1 medium parsnip
2 medium carrots
1 small floury potato,
  eg King Edward

A great purée for the winter months. Try adding some chopped fresh herbs to make it more interesting for your baby. Parsnips can be quite sweet and have a lovely nutty flavour, making this purée especially popular. You may need to thin this purée down slightly with breast milk or formula milk or cooled, boiled water before serving.

1 Peel and chop all the vegetables into small dice.
2 Put them into a steamer or colander over a pan of boiling water.
3 Cover with a lid and steam for 10 minutes, until all the vegetables are tender.
4 Allow to cool slightly before whizzing with a hand-held blender (or in a food processor or blender) until smooth.
5 Leave to cool before freezing.
6 Spoon the purée into ice-cube trays. Cover with foil or put into a freezer bag and seal. Freeze.
7 To serve, thaw thoroughly and then reheat.

swede and carrot purée

makes: 3 baby portions

storage: up to 2 months in the freezer

Vitamin A

1 small or ½ large swede
2 medium carrots

Swede is an often forgotten vegetable, but it has a lovely mellow taste that is popular with babies. Steaming swede helps to preserve its flavour, which may be lost if the vegetable is boiled. Try adding a little pinch of ginger or cinnamon, which will enhance it further.

1 Peel the vegetables and cut into small chunks.
2 Put into a steamer or colander over a pan of boiling water.
3 Cover with a lid and steam for 10 minutes, until all the vegetables are tender.
4 Allow to cool slightly before whizzing with a hand-held blender (or in a food processor or blender) until smooth.
5 Spoon the purée into ice-cube trays. Cover with foil or put into a freezer bag and seal. Freeze.
6 To serve, thaw thoroughly and then reheat.

brussels sprout and pea purée

makes: 3 baby portions

storage: up to 2 months in the freezer

15 small Brussels sprouts
100g peas, fresh or frozen

Big, old sprouts can be quite bitter and unpleasant tasting, so choose the smaller ones. Steaming sprouts will also help prevent them getting too watery. The peas give a lovely sweetness to the purée. Try adding some chopped herbs to make it a little more interesting for your baby.

1 Remove the outer leaves from the sprouts and cut off the base. Bring a pan of water to the boil and steam the sprouts until just tender (about 7 minutes).
2 A couple of minutes before the sprouts are cooked, add the peas to the boiling water and cook until just tender.
3 Drain and whiz the vegetables with a hand-held blender (or in a food processor or blender) until smooth. You may need to add 2-3 tsp cooled, boiled water to help blend the vegetables.
4 For just-weaned babies, pass the purée through a nylon sieve.
5 Spoon the purée into ice-cube trays. Cover with foil or put into a freezer bag and seal. Freeze.
6 To serve, thaw thoroughly and then reheat.

leek and courgette purée

makes: 4 baby portions

storage: up to 2 months in the freezer

1 medium leek
1 small courgette

Leeks are a member of the onion family, although they are considerably milder than onions. Look for medium-sized leeks (the old ones can be quite tough) that are tightly formed. Make sure you wash them really well – it's surprising how much grit they can contain. Leeks can cause wind in some babies, so introduce them gradually.

1 Remove the tough outer leaves of the leek and then trim off the ends. Slice the leek lengthways and clean under running water to remove any grit. Cut into chunks.
2 Slice the ends off the courgette and then cut the vegetable into chunks.
3 Put the leek slices and courgette chunks into a steamer or a colander over a pan of boiling water. Cover them with a lid and steam for 10 minutes, until they are tender.
4 Allow to cool slightly before whizzing with a hand-held blender (or in a food processor) until smooth. For just-weaned babies, push through a nylon sieve.
5 Spoon the purée into ice-cube trays. Cover with foil or put into a freezer bag and seal. Freeze.
6 To serve, thaw thoroughly and then reheat.

parsnip and potato purée

makes: 5 baby portions

storage: up to 2 months in the freezer

1 large or 2 small parsnips
1 medium floury potato,
  eg King Edward

This is a great early purée, with a really smooth texture and subtle, sweet flavour. As your baby gets used to it, try adding some chopped rosemary or, for the more adventurous, a little mild curry powder – it goes brilliantly.

1 Peel the vegetables and cut into small chunks.
2 Put into a steamer or colander over a pan of boiling water.
3 Cover with a lid and steam for 10 minutes, until all the vegetables are tender.
4 Allow to cool slightly before whizzing with a hand-held blender (or in a food processor or blender) until smooth. Add a few teaspoons of liquid.
5 Spoon the purée into ice-cube trays. Cover with foil or put into a freezer bag and seal. Freeze.
6 To serve, thaw thoroughly and then reheat and mix with a few teaspoons of breast milk, formula milk or cooled, boiled water.

broccoli and cauliflower purée

makes: 3 baby portions

storage: up to 2 months in the freezer

1 medium head of broccoli broken into florets

3 cauliflower florets

Broccoli is a member of the cabbage family, but it does not have such renowned wind-inducing properties! Broccoli is one of the most nutritious of all vegetables; it's rich in vitamin C, betacarotene, iron, and potassium. The darker the broccoli florets are, the more useful nutrients they contain, so make sure you choose ones that are tightly formed and a deep green – anything that has yellowed will not be good.

1 Remove all the tough stalks from the broccoli and the cauliflower and cut the florets into small chunks.
2 Put the broccoli and cauliflower into a steamer or colander over a pan of boiling water.
3 Cover with a lid and steam for 8 minutes, until the vegetables are tender.
4 Cool before whizzing with a hand-held blender (or in a food processor or blender) until it is smooth (it will take a few minutes to achieve a nice smooth purée).
5 Spoon the purée into ice-cube trays. Cover with foil or put into a freezer bag and seal. Freeze.
6 To serve, thaw thoroughly and then reheat.

pea and courgette purée

makes: 3 baby portions

storage: up to 2 months in the freezer

1 small courgette

100g peas, fresh or frozen

Unlike marrows, their larger relatives, courgettes have tender, edible skins, so as long as you use organic courgettes, your baby can benefit from the nutrients their skins contain. They are good sources of vitamin C and betacarotene. Choose courgettes that are firm and not too large or they will be watery and tasteless. A little chopped rosemary will help to bring out the flavour of the courgettes really well.

1 Cut the ends off the courgette and cut the vegetable into small chunks.
2 Steam the courgette and the peas for 3-4 minutes, until just tender. Alternatively, simmer gently until the vegetables are soft (about 5 minutes).
3 Drain and whiz with a hand-held blender (or in a food processor or blender) until smooth. For just-weaned babies, push through a nylon sieve.
4 Allow to cool before freezing.
5 Spoon the purée into ice-cube trays. Cover with foil or put into a freezer bag and seal. Freeze.
6 To serve, thaw thoroughly and then reheat.

fresh puddings

mango and fresh apricot purée

1½ **C**

makes: 3 baby portions or 1 baby portion and 1 adult portion as a smoothie base

storage: up to 24 hours in the refrigerator

1 ripe mango
2 fresh apricots

This is a gorgeous purée, and it's definitely worth making extra so you can have a smoothie yourself. Just add some apple or orange juice or coconut milk and a squeeze of lime.

1 Slice through the mango on either side of the stone. Peel, then cut the flesh into cubes.
2 Stone and peel the apricots and cut the flesh into small pieces.
3 Put the mango and chopped apricots into a pan. Add 4 tbsp water and cook gently until the mango has broken down and the apricot pieces are soft (approximately 5-10 minutes). Cool.
4 Whiz the fruits together with a hand-held blender (or in a food processor or blender) until smooth.
5 For a just-weaned baby, pass the purée through a nylon sieve.

apple and plum purée

1¼ **C**

makes: 2 baby portions

storage: up to 24 hours in the refrigerator

1 eating apple, eg Cox's orange pippin
1 ripe plum
pinch of ground cinnamon

Apples and plums are in season at the same time, making them a good match. You could always add a little pinch of ginger to this purée instead of cinnamon if you want extra spice, but because this is hotter, ginger might be more suitable for older babies.

1 Peel, core, and slice the apple. Peel and halve the plum, remove the stone, and chop the flesh into small pieces.
2 Put the apple and plum into a saucepan with 2 tbsp water and the cinnamon. Heat gently until the apple is soft and pulpy (approximately 5 minutes) stirring occasionally. Cool.
3 Whiz with a hand-held blender (or in a food processor or blender) until smooth.
4 For just-weaned babies, pass this purée through a nylon sieve.

Before feeding your baby any of these purées, please read the section on weaning (pages 42/43) and the 4-6 month sample meal planners (pages 48/49)

pear and blackcurrant purée

makes: 1 baby portion

storage: up to 24 hours in the refrigerator

1 ripe pear
handful of fresh ripe
blackcurrants

If you can't find fresh blackcurrants, use frozen. Pear and redcurrant is another delicious combination. If the blackcurrants are not quite ripe or are too sharp, add more pear. Blackcurrants are exceptionally rich in vitamin C, having four times as much as the equivalent weight of oranges.

1 Peel, core, and slice the pear.
2 Put the pear and blackcurrants into a saucepan with 1 tbsp water.
3 Heat gently until the pear is soft and pulpy and the blackcurrants have burst open (about 4-5 minutes).
4 Whiz with a hand-held blender (or in a food processor or blender) until smooth.
5 Push the purée through a sieve before serving.

nectarine and peach purée

makes: 2 baby portions or 1 baby portion and 1 small adult portion

storage: up to 24 hours in the refrigerator

1 ripe peach
1 ripe nectarine

Make this in the summer, when these fruits are plentiful. It's really not worth it at other times of the year because the fruit will be imported, and consequently expensive and often of poor quality.

1 Halve the peach and nectarine, remove their stones and chop the flesh into small pieces.
2 Put the fruit into a small saucepan with 2 tbsp water and cook gently until it is soft and pulpy (approximately 5 minutes). Cool.
3 Whiz the fruits together with a hand-held blender (or in a food processor or blender) until smooth.
4 For a just-weaned baby, pass the purée through a nylon sieve.

mango and melon purée

makes: 3 baby portions or 1 baby portion and 1 adult portion as a smoothie base

storage: up to 24 hours in the refrigerator

1 ripe mango
½ small ripe melon, eg Galia

Mangoes are a great source of nutrients. When they are cheap, cook and then whiz up lots of the pulp and freeze in ice-cube trays, then add to purées, smoothies and breakfast cereals. All forms of melon are mildly laxative.

1 Slice through the mango on either side of the stone. Peel, then cut the flesh into cubes.
2 Cut the melon in half, scoop the seeds out, and separate the skin from the flesh. Cut the flesh into small cubes.
3 Put the mango and melon in a pan with 2-3 tbsp water a cook for a few minutes, until soft.
4 Whiz the fruits using a hand-held blender (or in a food processor or blender) until smooth. For a just-weaned baby, pass the purée through a nylon sieve.

blueberry and banana purée

makes: 2 baby portions or 1 baby portion and 1 small adult portion as a smoothie base

storage: up to 24 hours in the refrigerator

150g blueberries
pinch of ground cinnamon
1 small ripe banana

The starch in bananas is not very easy for babies to digest, but when bananas are ripe most of the starch has turned to sugar. This is why it is so important to choose ripe bananas for all baby food – look for those with little brown specks all over the skin. A little spice, such as cinnamon, can be introduced once your baby has been taking solids for at least a month. So, either serve this purée with or without the cinnamon; you decide if your baby is ready for a new taste.

1 Put the blueberries and cinnamon into a small saucepan with 3 tbsp water. Heat gently until the berries are just beginning to burst. Cool.
2 Whiz the blueberries and banana together using a hand-held blender (or in a food processor or blender) until smooth.
3 For a just-weaned baby, pass the purée through a nylon sieve.

quick bites fruit purées

You may need to add breast milk, or formula milk or a baby rice to these purées to make the desired consistency.

Vitamin A

makes 2 portions
1 ripe mango

mango

Mango is naturally sweet and easy to digest. Rich in vitamin C, minerals, and antioxidants, it is great for the immune system and for convalescing babies. Choose ripe mangoes; unripe ones can cause stomach upsets. Peel the fruit, then wash the peeling knife before chopping. Slice the mango down each side of the stone. Scoop out the flesh using a spoon (if you can't do this the fruit is probably not ripe enough). Steam or simmer in 2-3 tbsp water for a few minutes, until soft. Whiz with a hand-held blender (or in a food processor or blender) until smooth. Mangoes can be stringy and need passing through a nylon sieve.

1 medium eating apple

apple

When cooked, apples' sweet, soft purée is always popular with babies. Apples are rich in antioxidants, so they are a good immune-boosting food. They are also good for diarrhoea and constipation. Buy organic, tree-ripened apples. Peel and core the apple. Cut it into small pieces and simmer in water or steam for 5 minutes, until soft. Whiz with a hand-held blender (or in a food processor or blender) until smooth. You can also bake apples. Cut the fruit in half and scoop out the core. Score a line around its middle and bake at 180°C/350°F/gas mark 4–25 minutes, until soft. Scoop the flesh from the skin and mash.

1 medium ripe banana

banana

Bananas are a great first food, but the purée can be a bit thick for a baby to swallow, so add a little boiled water or breast or formula milk. Buy really ripe fruit, as the starch will have turned to sugar, making it easier on a baby's delicate digestive system. Bananas are also good for diarrhoea and constipation. Peel your bananas and mash or purée. Dilute it with water or breast or formula milk as necessary. Alternatively, bake a banana in its skin for 20 minutes at 180°C/350°F/gas mark 4. Cool and peel, then mash the flesh.

blueberry

handful of blueberries

Blueberries can be hard for babies to digest, so they are best puréed and sieved or put through a mouli until weaning has been underway for at least four months. Blueberries have natural antibacterial properties, which help to prevent mild colds and they are also excellent for treating diarrhoea. Put the blueberries in a saucepan with a little water and simmer gently until the fruit bursts open. Whiz with a hand-held blender (or in a food processor or blender) until smooth. For just-weaned babies, pass the purée through a nylon sieve.

cherry

handful of cherries

Cherries have good cleansing and antioxidant properties, which make them great for building up resistance. They are also good for constipation. They have high levels of vitamin C, potassium, and magnesium. Stone your cherries, then cook them in a small pan with a little water. When they are soft, cool and then whiz with a hand-held blender (or in a food processor or blender) until smooth. For just-weaned babies, pass the purée through a nylon sieve.

apricot

1 apricot

Apricots are rich in betacarotene, which the body converts into vitamin A. They are good for constipation – especially dried apricots, but these are best given to babies over 6 months. Apricots also have high levels of iron and potassium. First skin your fruit by putting it in boiling water. Leave for 1 minute, then slip the skin off using a sharp knife. Finely chop and cook with 1 tbsp water until soft. Whiz with a hand-held blender (or in a food processor or blender) until smooth.

melon

chunk of melon

Cantaloupe, galia, and charentais are the sweetest varieties. Melons are good for digestion, but are also a mild laxative. Simmer the melon with a little water for a few minutes, until soft. When buying melon, choose ones that feel heavy for their size and have a sweet aroma. Peel your melon and remove the seeds. Whiz with a hand-held blender (or in a food processor or blender) until smooth.

pear

1 ripe pear

Pears are a great first food because they have a fairly neutral flavour. They relieve constipation and are good for convalescence. Peel and core your pear and cut into bite-size pieces. Cook gently in a small pan with a little water until soft. Whiz with a hand-held blender (or in a food processor or blender) until smooth.

All quick bites make 1 portion unless otherwise stated.

puddings to freeze

raspberry and apple purée

makes: 3 baby portions

storage: up to 2 months in the freezer

3 eating apples, eg Cox's orange pippin
150g raspberries

Use fresh raspberries when they are in season; otherwise frozen ones are just as good, especially if you buy organic. This is also delicious stirred through some natural yogurt as a pudding or breakfast for mum. If your baby is used to spice, try adding a pinch of cinnamon, as it really brings out the flavour of both the apples and the raspberries.

1 Peel and core the apples, then cut into bite-sized pieces. Put them into a small pan with 6 tbsp water and cook gently until the apples are just beginning to soften (approximately 10-15 minutes).
2 Add the raspberries to the pan and cook for a further 3 minutes. Remove from the heat and cool.
3 Whiz the fruits using a hand-held blender (or in a food processor or blender) until smooth.
4 For a just-weaned baby, pass the purée through a nylon sieve.
5 Spoon the purée into ice-cube trays. Cover with foil or put into a freezer bag and seal. Freeze.
6 To serve, thaw thoroughly.

blueberry purée

makes: 3 baby portions

storage: up to 24 hours in refrigerator

1 ripe pear, eg Williams
4-5 tbsp water
50g blueberries

Before feeding your baby any of these purées, please read the section on weaning (pages 42/43) and the 4-6 month sample meal planners (pages 48/49)

Just a hint of spice is a good thing occasionally to get your baby's palate used to different flavours.

1 Peel and core the pear and cut it into bite-sized chunks.
2 Put the pear into a saucepan with the water and blueberries.
3 Simmer for a few minutes, until the pear is tender and the blueberries have just burst open (it won't take long).
4 Whiz with a hand-held blender or in a food processor or blender until smooth. Leave to cool before serving. For just-weaned babies, sieve the purée using a nylon sieve. Freeze.
5 To serve, thaw thoroughly.

parsnip and apple purée

makes: 2 baby portions

storage: up to 2 months in the freezer

1 small parsnip
1 ripe apple

Parsnips are a naturally sweet vegetable, and apples complement their flavour really well. This delicious purée makes a great winter treat for young babies.

1 Peel the parsnip and cut it into small dice. Cook it in a small pan of boiling water until the pieces are just tender. Alternatively, steam over a pan of boiling water. Drain.

2 Peel and core the apple and cut it into small pieces. Put it into a small pan with 2 tbsp water and cook until just softened.

3 Whiz the parsnip and apple together with a hand-held blender or in a food processor or blender until smooth. Freeze.

4 To serve, thaw thoroughly.

pear and blackberry purée

makes: 2 baby portions

storage: up to 2 months in the freezer

2 ripe pears
100g blackberries

This is definitely one for the blackberry season, although you could use the same weight of mixed frozen fruits instead if necessary. Ripe blackberries are one of the least tart of all the berries, and mixed with pears they make an excellent weaning food. While pears are great because they have a taste and texture babies love, be aware that they can make some babies quite windy.

1 Peel and core the pears, then cut them into bite-size pieces. Put them into a small saucepan with the blackberries and 2 tbsp water.

2 Heat gently until the pear is soft and the blackberries are giving up their juice (approximately 5-10 minutes, depending on how ripe they are). Cool.

3 Whiz the fruits using a hand-held blender (or in a food processor or blender) until smooth.

4 For a just-weaned baby, pass the purée through a nylon sieve.

5 Spoon the purée into ice-cube trays. Cover with foil or put into a freezer bag and seal. Freeze.

6 To serve, thaw thoroughly.

peach and cherry purée

makes: 3 baby portions

storage: up to 2 months in the freezer

3 ripe peaches
handful of cherries

A really summery pudding – make the most of the fruits while they are in season and then pop the pudding in the freezer.

1 Cut the peaches in half, remove the stones, then chop flesh into small pieces.
2 Stone the cherries over a clean bowl to catch all the juices. Put in a pan with the peach flesh and cook in 1-2 tbsp water for a few minutes, until soft.
3 Whiz with a hand-held blender (or in a food processor or blender) until smooth.
4 For a just-weaned baby, push the fruit through a nylon sieve until smooth.
5 Spoon the purée into ice-cube trays. Cover with foil or put into a freezer bag and seal. Freeze.
6 To serve, thaw thoroughly.

pear and carrot purée

makes: 2 baby portions

storage: up to 2 months in the freezer

1 small carrot
1 ripe pear

Pears are particularly good if you think your baby may be slightly constipated – if you are still breastfeeding, try drinking some pear juice yourself if your baby is constipated; it really seems to do the trick.

1 Peel the carrot and cut into small dice. Cook in a small pan of boiling water until the pieces are just tender (approximately 3-4 minutes). Alternatively, steam over a pan of boiling water (approximately 5 minutes). Drain.
2 Peel and core the pear and cut into small pieces. Put them into a small pan with 2 tbsp water and cook until just softened (approximately 5 minutes), depending on the pear's ripeness.
3 Whiz the pear and carrot together with a hand-held blender (or in a food processor or blender) until smooth.
4 Spoon the purée into ice-cube trays. Cover with foil or put into a freezer bag and seal. Freeze.
5 To serve, thaw thoroughly.

At this stage in her life, your baby goes through a period of rapid growth and development. Milk will still provide most of the nutrients she needs, but solid food will become more important. As she gets more used to solids, you can start to vary tastes and textures. Her physiological development will aid the weaning process – she will have better hand–eye co-ordination, so she will be able to steer hand-held foods towards her mouth while she sits unaided. She may start to teethe, which will help her to cope with lumpier food. This stage is about encouraging her to enjoy food, which will help to form the basis of healthy eating habits that can last a lifetime.

7-9
months

what's happening to
your baby

Your baby will now be more alert, especially visually, and she will take far more notice of things around her. She will be begin to be selective about the people around her and may be wary of strangers. She will sleep less during the day and will gradually become more active. She will be more mobile and able to roll over onto her tummy, lift her head, sit unsupported, and perhaps stand while being held or hold on to pieces of furniture. She will be able to wave hello and goodbye and may even be able to crawl. You will become increasingly aware of her babbling because she starts to make more recognizable sounds, such as ga-ga, ma-ma, and da-da. Now is a good time to introduce a few simple games; for example, show her a picture of a cow, say "moo", and watch her response.

eating and drinking

Your baby's coordination will be much improved, and she will be able to move objects from hand to hand and hand to mouth. Her teeth may be developing, and she will have learned how to swallow food rather than suck it from a spoon. Her appetite will increase as she becomes more active, and she will see other people eating and drinking and want to imitate them. She is ready for new eating experiences. Try to feed her some meals at the same time as the rest of the family eats, so that she feels she belongs and can copy what other family members are doing.

Your baby will be receptive to a wide range of tastes and textures now; even mildly spiced food might be accepted, if only on the third try. Her taste buds will really develop over a six to eight week period. It is important to give your baby lots of different foods at this stage, especially foods with stronger flavours – for example, vegetables such as carrots, broccoli, spinach, turnip, and avocado, and white fish and lean meat. After this development period, especially as she becomes more aware, she will have acquired strong preferences for certain foods, and introducing new flavours will become more difficult – particularly if you have fed your baby only ready-prepared baby foods, which are often bland.

Different babies develop at different rates, and only you will know at what point your baby is likely to be confident with chewing. At this stage of her development, your baby is likely to progress from puréed to mashed food and possibly to chunks of food, depending on her teeth and confidence with chewing. The most important thing is, never leave a baby alone while feeding.

Breast milk is still the primary source of nutrition for your baby, but the nutrients she gets from solids are becoming more important. Up to this point, you will have fed your baby only fruits, vegetables, and baby rice. As she starts to stay awake for longer periods she will need more food. Give foods that are nutrient-dense and high in energy, such as finely ground nuts and seeds and oils (do not give nuts to babies if there is a family history of food allergies). Foods that are high in carbohydrates should also be added to her diet. A good source of protein will be needed. Iron is especially important at this stage, too, as babies are born with a natural store of this nutrient which becomes depleted at around 6 months old.

vegetarian and vegan babies

Follow the same basic rules as any mum (see pages 12-19), paying particular attention to:

Protein – good sources include beans, cereals, pulses, finely ground nuts and seeds (do not feed nuts to babies if there is any history of food allergies) and tofu.

Iron – good sources include bread, pulses, green vegetables and chopped dried fruit.

Calcium – dairy produce can be given in small quantities at this age. Good sources for a vegan diet are green vegetables, chopped dried fruits, ground nuts and fortified foods such as bread.

Iodine – good sources include grains and vegetables. You may also like to include an iodine supplement. Speak to your family doctor or state-registered dietician for more information.

Vitamin D – this is made in your baby's skin when she's exposed to sunlight, so make sure that your baby has at least half an hour outside every day. Vegetarian babies can have a little dairy produce, which will boost their vitamin D. Vegan babies should be given vegan margarine, which is fortified with vitamin D.

Vitamin B2 – ground wholegrain cereals, leafy green vegetables and ground almonds.

Anyone considering providing their baby with a vegan diet should consult a state-registered dietician.

which nutrients **are key**

nutrients required per day

Milk provides your baby with much of her nutritional needs from 7 to 9 months – for this book we've assumed the lowest level provided by the common brands on which the milk chart on page 21 is based. If you're successfully breast-feeding, your baby should get at least these levels from your milk.
* If you feed your baby a healthy balanced diet of fresh food, you will almost certainly give her much more protein and vitamin C than she needs. Do not worry, as this will not damage her health at these levels.

	protein 1 point = 1.5 grams	iron 1 point = 1.5mg	zinc 1 point = 1mg	calcium 1 point = 105mg	vitamin C 1 point = 5mg
total points recommended	9 (13.7g)	5 (7.8mg)	5 (5g)	5 (525mg)	5 (25mg)
milk (700ml of formula) provides	6½ (9.8g)	2½ (3.5mg)	3½ (3.5mg)	3 (322mg)	11½(57.4mg)
points required from food	2½ (*see caption)	2½	1½	2	0 (*see caption)

second-stage
weaning

The purpose of this stage of weaning is to establish a regular eating pattern and to increase the range of nutritionally rich foods you give your baby, so that her solids will become her main source of nutrients rather than breast milk. Once you feel that your baby is comfortable eating three meals a day, with finger foods and water in-between, you can start to offer breast milk or formula milk as an after-solids drink only. This is best begun first thing in the morning, when your baby will be at her hungriest. You can take advantage of this, and hopefully she will eat more solids. Gradually, breakfast can become the largest meal of the day.

New foods

As your baby learns to swallow and chew and her teeth grow, you can gradually introduce new foods. It's important to remember that babies develop at different paces, and that some babies will be comfortable with new foods earlier than others. They key thing is that they should never be left alone with food at any time. Try foods that have a coarser texture; mince or mash purées rather than blending them, but always wash and peel fruit and vegetables and remove pips.

As your baby's digestive system matures and her appetite increases, you can add many more foods to her diet. Fish, lean meat, and poultry should be offered at least once a week to increase her protein and iron intake. (Always check fish for bones, then grill or poach, and always mash the cooked food.) Babies can find the flavour of protein strong when a food is cooked on its own, so try mixing it with a blander food such as potato.

Iron is particularly important at this stage (see page 87). If your baby is being given a vegan diet and is relying on pulses such as beans and lentils for protein, she will need iron from other sources too, such as green vegetables, especially broccoli, spinach and watercress, and puréed cooked dried fruit such as prunes and unsulphured apricots. Always make sure pulses are thoroughly cooked, because they are high in fibre and can be hard for babies to digest. Similarly, avoid giving babies high-fibre breakfast cereals at this stage because their digestive systems will not be able to cope.

Towards the end of this age group, if your baby is confident with chewing you can introduce wheat and wheat-based foods, such as pasta and cereals. These are great for encouraging babies to chew and use their jaw muscles. Bread, bread sticks, and unsalted rice cakes can also be cut into finger-size pieces – but check their labels for salt and sugar content before you buy. At this stage babies love finger foods; try pieces of ripe soft peeled fruit or cooked soft vegetables. Chop these foods large enough to hold and chew on, rather than bite-size to minimize the risk of choking – and always keep an eye on her. Now that your baby is having finger foods always wash her hands before her meals.

Small amounts of full-fat cow's milk can be given if incorporated into a dish rather than as a drink. And it is important to give your baby cooled, boiled tap water between meals.

Allergic reactions

Occasionally, harmless foods such as nuts or cow's milk, can be perceived as aggressive by a baby's immune system. This triggers an allergic reaction. Some reactions cause mild discomfort, while others can be life-threatening. Allergies in children, particularly asthma and eczema, are on the increase. Seek advice from your family doctor or a state-registered dietician or registered nutritionist.

7-9 months: common myths

myth: eating utensils must be sterilized
Up to the age of 7 months, sterilize all of your baby's eating utensils (see page 29). After 7 months, just wash and rinse them well and allow them to air-dry.

myth: low fat diets are good
It is more important to make sure babies get a wide variety of foods and enough energy for their rapid development than to worry about their fat intake.

myth: high fibre diets are good
A fibre-rich diet can be detrimental to your baby's health. Her stomach capacity is too small for most high-fibre meals. Fibre can also hinder the absorption of nutrients.

myth: ready-made baby foods are better
While ready-prepared baby foods have their uses, there is no substitute for real food. Its nutrient content is far superior and, although home-made purées will have a coarser texture or less consistent flavour, this will help to instil in your baby an appreciation for fresh food with real flavours.

myth: allergies are common in babies
If you introduce foods at the correct stage, there is no reason why your baby should have an adverse reaction unless there is a history of allergy in your family. Do not restrict your baby's diet by cutting out food on the basis of unproven tests or without expert advice.

foods to eat and
foods to avoid

new foods to eat at 7-9 months

It's important to remember that babies develop at different paces, and will learn to chew at different rates, so only you will know. They should never be left alone with food at any time.

- Mashed lean meat, poultry and fish (except shellfish) at least once a week; avoid salty/smoked food.
- Pulses, such as lentils, chickpeas, haricot beans, flageolet beans and kidney beans.
- Later on, wheat or wheat-based foods, such as pasta and sugar-free unrefined cereals.
- Small amounts of full-fat dairy produce, such as natural yogurt, a little well-cooked egg, pasteurized cheese, or calcium-enriched soya dairy alternatives to milk, yogurt and desserts.
- Citrus fruits – but mix with other fruits to counteract their sugar and acid content.
- Puréed dried fruits can be introduced gradually. Mix with other fruits because they might cause an upset stomach.
- Water, boiled and cooled, as a drink between meals.
- Finely ground nuts and smooth nut butters, assuming there is no family history of allergies.

foods to avoid at 7-9 months

- Cow's milk should not be given as a drink, although small amounts can be used in meals. Milk can be one of the most residue-contaminated foods, so I would always use organic milk.
- Shellfish can trigger allergic reactions. Avoid until your child is at least 2 years old.
- Unpasteurized cheese may contain the bacteria listeria, which can cause food-poisoning.
- Soft-boiled eggs and runny yolks may contain the food-poisoning bacteria salmonella, to which babies are far more sensitive than adults. Eggs should always be hard boiled.
- Salt cannot be processed by a baby's immature digestive system; it causes dehydration. A diet high in salt often leads to high blood pressure. Particular foods to avoid at this stage are yeast extracts such as marmite or vegemite and stock cubes. Most food labels refer to salt as sodium.
- Refined or unrefined sugar provides calories but few nutrients. It's a major cause of tooth decay and can lead to health problems such as obesity. It is not necessary to add sugar to your baby's food. Check labels because sugar may be present as sucrose, glucose, fructose, lactose, hydrolyzed starch, invert sugar, and products such as treacle, honey, and golden syrup.
- Never give your baby artificial sweeteners.
- Honey may contain botulism spores which can cause food poisoning, and this is far more serious in babies than it is in adults.
- Avoid excessively hot or spicy foods, which can burn or inflame babies' stomachs.
- Tea and coffee contain tannins that inhibit iron absorption. Babies cannot tolerate caffeine.

recommended
daily intake

Breast milk or formula milk continue to be the primary source of nutrition for your baby when she is 7-9 months old. However, the nutrients that are provided by solid food are becoming more and more important to her, and this is the time to establish a routine in which your baby eats three meals a day, with finger foods and cooled, boiled tap water in-between those meals.

Until now, you have mostly offered your baby breast milk or formula milk before giving her any solid food, in order to ensure that she drinks it all and gets all of the nutrients she needs. Now you can start to offer breast milk or formula milk as an after-solids drink only. Begin by doing this at breakfast time, when your baby will be at her hungriest and so (hopefully) will eat more solids. Eventually breakfast can become the largest meal of the day.

This is also the time for introducing lots of new foods to your baby's diet. Until now, she has eaten mainly fruit, vegetables, and baby rice. See pages 86-90 for details of foods to introduce. Use the chart below as a guide to how much to feed your baby each day, remembering that all babies have quite different needs, depending on many factors, including weight. You will have to follow your baby's direction and use your own initiative when deciding how much to feed her each day.

recommended daily volume of foods

milk = breastfeed or approx 200ml formula

	7 months old	**8 months old**	**9 months old**
Breakfast 7-8am	1 portion breakfast, then milk	1 portion breakfast, then milk	1-2 portions breakfast, then milk
Lunch 11.45-ish	1 portion lunch, alternating during feed with milk, gradually changing from milk to cooled boiled water or very well-diluted juice from a cup	1 portion lunch plus drink of cooled boiled water or well-diluted fruit juice from a cup	1 portion lunch plus occasionally 1 small portion fruit purée or healthy snack with drink of cooled boiled water or very well-diluted juice from a cup
Mid-pm, 3pm	milk	milk	milk
Supper 6.30pm-ish	1 portion supper plus occasionally 1 portion pudding plus cooled boiled water or well-diluted fruit juice from a cup, then milk, in bed by 7pm-ish	1 portion supper plus occasionally 1 portion pudding plus cooled boiled water or well-diluted fruit juice from a cup, then milk, in bed by 7pm-ish	1 portion supper plus occasionally 1 portion pudding plus cooled boiled water or well-diluted fruit juice from a cup, then milk, in bed by 7pm-ish
Night-time 10pm	small milk feed if needed	small milk feed if needed	small milk feed if needed
TOTAL MILK	breast milk or 600-700ml formula, depending on baby size, inclusive of milk used in sauces, cereals	breast milk or 600-700ml formula, depending on baby size, inclusive of milk used in sauces, cereals	breast milk or 600-700ml formula, depending on baby size, inclusive of milk used in sauces, cereals

your
routine

your baby's feeds

Solids are becoming more important because milk cannot provide all the nutrients your baby now needs. To help her to eat the right amount of solids, you will need to reduce some of her milk feeds gradually. The best way to start is to reduce the amount of milk she drinks at lunch. Keep alternating food and milk during the lunchtime feed until you feel she is ready to have just solid foods with a drink of water. By 7 months, she should be eating supper with a drink of water and having her milk feed later, just before bed.

I love this stage because it is a time when you can begin to offer foods that your baby can hold and feed to herself. Finger foods help your baby feel a little more independent, and they can help to keep her interested in food: its shapes, colours and textures. By 9 months, it is also worth aiming to give her all of her drinks, other than milk, in a beaker. This will help when you come to stopping the bottle later on.

your baby's sleeps

Most babies at this age still need a quick nap after breakfast for up to 45 minutes. However, she may be ready to cut this sleep out. If you would like to encourage this, you may like to feed her lunch slightly earlier so that her after-lunch sleep is a little earlier; she'll still need at least a couple of hours at lunchtime. Then, when she is used to lasting the morning, you can gradually move lunchtime back again to a time that fits in with the rest of the family.

I remember feeling quite excited when Ella and Jasmin were only having one sleep during the day; it made life quite a lot easier if I wanted to go out and about. The important thing is to not make any changes that affect the night sleep. You need to try and keep her sleeping through, for your sake as much as hers. If she does start to wake up during the night, you may want to offer water instead of milk to discourage it from becoming a habit. If she is eating well during the day, she should not need any more food at night-time.

when teething affects your baby's eating pattern

When teeth start to grow through your baby's gums, the pressure can cause some discomfort and may even affect her eating patterns. Most babies love to suck and chew things when teething so this is an ideal time to introduce finger foods.

involving your baby in feeding

Give your baby a piece of finger food or a spoon dipped in a purée to encourage independence and help her become more coordinated. Letting her chew and suck a spoon will also help her get used to the feel of it in her mouth.

no enjoyment of mealtimes

Most families talk at the table – it makes mealtimes far more enjoyable. Talking to your baby while you are feeding her encourages enthusiasm about mealtimes. Even saying things like "yum yum" or congratulating her when she has managed to eat something will have positive effects.

no interest in food

Try to give your baby your undivided attention when you are feeding so she doesn't lose interest in the food.

if your baby dislikes a food

There will be some foods your baby does not like – every baby has different tastes. If a particular purée is not a hit, try it again a few days later. Some purées, especially vegetables such as beetroot or cauliflower, can have quite intense flavours, so try diluting them with baby rice, potato or breast milk or formula milk to make them more palatable.

avoiding dehydration

Always make sure your baby has plenty of water to drink. The fluid will prevent constipation, which can occur when solid foods are increased. Babies can now be encouraged to drink cooled, boiled water, given in a "first cup". The best way to do this is to offer it consistently at the same time each day, for example at lunch, and between every few mouthfuls of food. You may need to experiment with different types of cups to see which one your baby prefers.

a full baby

Your baby will close her mouth and turn her head away when she is full. Never try to force her to eat more than she wants. Respect her appetite.

trouble
shooting

sample meal planners

key to meal planners

each milk feed:
Breastfeed or 200ml formula milk

portions:
After 5 months, all servings of food referred to in the meal planners is 1 portion

water:
Always give cooled, boiled water or very diluted fruit juice. After 9 month, all drinks should be served in a beaker.

mealtimes:
breakfast 7-8am
lunch 11.45-ish
mid-afternoon 3pm
supper 6.30pm-ish, for bed at 7pm-ish

At 7-9 months, solids start to become a more important source of nutrition. On page 87 you'll find a chart showing how much of each of the key nutrients your child generally needs to obtain from solid food. For some of these nutrients, in particular vitamin C and protein, you'll inevitably exceed these recommended intakes if you cook your baby fresh food; do not worry, as this will not harm your child. Equally, do not worry if your baby doesn't get enough points every single day, as all babies have cranky days. The important thing is to ensure that, on average, your baby is getting the recommended intake. If your baby is getting a good variety and mix of foods, all other essential nutrients that haven't been allocated points should be more than covered.

The key thing you need to achieve at mealtimes during these months is a regular eating pattern of three meals a day. Once your baby is comfortable with this, with snacks and water in between, you can offer milk after solids rather than before. Once your child starts to teethe and becomes more confident with chewing, you can begin to offer her coarser-textured foods. Your baby's digestive system will be more developed now, as well as her teeth, so you can introduce many new foods (see page 90).

7 months old, any week

	breakfast	lunch	mid-pm	supper	10pm
day 1	milk, then strawberry, apple and mint purée, water	guacamole, water	milk and water	creamy mushroom pasta sauce, water, milk	small milk if needed
day 2	milk, then strawberry, apple and mint purée, water	minestrone, water	milk and water	sweet potato and coconut curry, water, milk	small milk if needed
day 3	milk, then vanilla porridge, water	potato purée, sweetcorn and carrot, water	milk and water	creamy tomato soup, water, milk	small milk if needed
day 4	milk, then fruity muesli, water	ratatouille, water	milk and water	baked pot with 2 cheeses, dried fruit, water, milk	small milk if needed
day 5	milk, then plum yogurt with muesli, water	poached fish with spinach sauce, water	milk and water	couscous with tomato and mozzarella, mango and banana fool, water, milk	small milk if needed
day 6	milk, then papaya and rice, water	courgette and mint purée, water	milk and water	salmon, broccoli and pasta, water, milk	small milk if needed
day 7	milk, then apple and banana purée, water	tomato and aubergine beef, water	milk and water	potato salad, water, milk	small milk if needed

8 months old, any week

	breakfast	lunch	mid-pm	supper	10pm
day 1	milk, banana and peach smoothie, toast, water	baked potato with 2 cheeses, water	milk and water	lamb with butternut squash, water, milk	small milk if needed
day 2	milk, then fruity muesli, water	chicken with sesame seeds, water	milk and water	bubble and squeak with cheese, water, milk	small milk if needed
day 3	milk, then mango lassi, water	creamy tomato soup, water	milk and water	salmon and broccoli pasta, mango and banana fool; water, milk	small milk if needed
day 4	milk, then papaya and rice, water	fruity Moroccan chicken, peach yogurt, water	milk and water	sweet potato and coconut curry, water, milk	small milk if needed
day 5	fruity muesli, water, then milk	minestrone, water	milk and water	macaroni and cauliflower cheese, rice pudding with blueberries, water, milk	small milk if needed
day 6	peach and cinnamon purée, water, then milk	creamy mushroom and pasta sauce, water	milk and water	butterbean/carrot paté, choc b&b pud, water, milk	small milk if needed
day 7	apricot and vanilla purée, water, then milk	tomato and aubergine beef, water	milk and water	tomato and mozzarella couscous, water, milk	small milk if needed

9 months old, any week

	breakfast	lunch	mid-pm	supper	10pm
day 1	plum yogurt with muesli, water, then milk	fruity Moroccan chicken, water	milk and water	peanut butter soliders; vegetable sticks, water	small milk if needed
day 2	mango, kiwi and banana puree, water, then milk	bubble and squeak with cheese, peach yogurt, water	milk and water	creamy tomato soup, water	small milk if needed
day 3	pear and apple muffins, water, then milk	potato salad, mango and peach purée, water	milk and water	chicken with sesame seeds, water	small milk if needed
day 4	raisin bread in milk with banana, water, then milk	mushrooms with tuna, water	milk and water	fish with spinach sauce, pear/almond yog, water	small milk if needed
day 5	papaya and rice, water, then milk	sweetcorn and potato soup, muesli bar, water	milk and water	salmon, brocolli and pasta, water	small milk if needed
day 6	prune and banana porridge, water, then milk	herby tomato pasta sauce with water	milk and water	fish fingers with carrot, banana teabread, water	small milk if needed
day 7	apricot couscous, water, then milk	quick pizza, pear and blackcurrant purée, water	milk and water	macaroni and cauliflower cheese, water	small milk if needed

fresh **breakfasts**

vanilla porridge

3

makes: 3 baby portions or 1 baby portion and 1 adult portion

½

storage: best eaten immediately or up to 24 hours in the refrigerator

1

½

½ **vanilla pod**

1+
200ml breast milk or formula milk

125ml water

60g oats

1 tbsp finely chopped or puréed mango

Vanilla is another flavour that babies seem to love and it is a really easy way to make porridge a little more interesting. Ella, my eldest, who is 3, still loves eating sugar-free vanilla porridge.

1 Split the vanilla pod lengthways.
2 Put all the ingredients into a saucepan and heat gently for 5 minutes, stirring often, until the mixture has thickened. Remove the vanilla pod.
3 Purée with a hand-blender (or in a food processor or blender), adding more milk or cooled, boiled water to create a runnier consistency if necessary.
4 If wished, serve with finely chopped or puréed mango, depending on your baby's confidence with chewing

strawberry, apple and mint purée

1

makes: 3 baby portions or 1 baby portion and 1 adult portion as a smoothie base or cereal topping

½

4 C
storage: best eaten immediately

handful of strawberries
½ small eating apple,
   eg Cox's orange pippin
1 mint leaf

Mint goes really well with strawberries, but try adding it to other fruit purées, too, especially melon. This is a great purée to give a baby who may be constipated, because strawberries are rich in both soluble and insoluble fibre, which help to relieve the condition.

1 Hull the strawberries.
2 Peel and core the apple, then roughly chop. Put it into a small saucepan with 2 tbsp water and heat gently until the apple is soft and pulpy.
3 Cool, then add the strawberries and the mint. Whiz with a hand-held blender (or in a food processor or blender) until smooth.

Note: not all recipes in this section are suitable for all babies in the age group. Please read the introductions carefully before serving them

plum yogurt with muesli

makes: 2 baby portions

storage: best eaten immediately or up to 24 hours in the refrigerator

1 ripe plum, eg Victoria or greengage
a tiny pinch ground ginger
2 tbsp natural full-fat yogurt
1 tbsp ground baby muesli
breast milk or formula milk, to serve

Small amounts of spices can be added to lots of different purées, not only to make them more interesting to your baby but also to educate her palate. It is at this early stage that a lifetime's eating habits can be influenced, so be bold! You could also include a little fresh grated ginger instead of ground ginger. Avoid muesli that contains nuts if there is any family history of allergies.

1 Remove the plum's stone and roughly chop.
2 Put the plum in a saucepan with the ginger and 2 tbsp water and heat gently until the plum is soft. Leave to cool.
3 Mash the plum into a purée, then add the yogurt, muesli and enough breast milk or formula milk to create the desired consistency. Mix together well.

prune and banana porridge

makes: 3 baby portions or 1 baby portion and 1 adult portion

storage: best eaten immediately or up to 24 hours in the refrigerator

Vitamin B$_{12}$

125ml boiling water
2 prunes, stoned and finely chopped (only for 9-month-old babies plus)
200ml breast milk or formula milk
60g oats
½ ripe medium banana, roughly chopped

A great purée for any older baby who is prone to constipation, because prunes are a natural laxative. But dried fruits can be difficult to digest, so I'd advise keeping this one for babies in their 9th month plus. As with all fruit for babies, make sure the bananas are ripe – they should have black spots. Unripe bananas can be indigestible for babies, as well as causing wind.

1 Pour the boiling water over the prunes and then leave them to soak for half an hour.
2 Put the soaked prunes in a pan with all the other ingredients except the banana, and then heat gently for 5 minutes, stirring often, until the mixture has thickened.
3 Add the banana and purée with a hand-blender (or in a food processor or blender), adding a little more milk or cooled, boiled water, to thin, if necessary.

mango, kiwi and banana purée

makes: 3 baby portions or 1 baby portion and 1 adult portion as a smoothie base

storage: best eaten immediately

½ ripe mango
1 ripe kiwi fruit
1 small ripe banana

This is a really zingy purée, but try adding a little bit of lime juice to help bring out the flavours of the fruit and give the purée an extra kick. Surprisingly, lots of older babies and toddlers really enjoy the sour taste of citrus fruits. My 3-year-old daughter, Ella, loves to suck on slices of lemon.

1   Remove the peel from the mango and then roughly chop the flesh into small pieces.
2   Peel and roughly chop the kiwi fruit and banana.
3   Put the fruit into a bowl and whiz with a hand-held blender (or in a food processor or blender) until smooth.

apple and banana purée

makes: 2 baby portions

storage: best eaten immediately or up to 24 hours in the refrigerator

75ml boiling water
1 small eating apple,
  eg Cox's orange pippin
1 small ripe banana, roughly chopped

This simple purée is always a favourite with babies, who love the taste of banana and the sweetness of apple.

1   Peel and core the apple, then chop into small pieces. Put it in a pan with a little boiling water and simmer gently until the apple is soft and pulpy (approximately 5 minutes), adding a little more water if necessary. Cool.
2   Whiz the banana and apple mixture together using a hand-held blender (or in a food processor or blender) until smooth.

quick bites breakfasts

6 **C** 1 🥚
melon and raspberry fruit salad

¼ ripe melon, eg Ogen
good handful of raspberries

Deseed, peel and finely chop the melon. Finely chop the raspberries. Mix the fruits together and mash with a fork or potato masher.

½ **C** ½ 🥚
apple yogurt

makes **2** portions
1 eating apple
2 tbsp natural full-fat yogurt

Peel, core and grate the apple. Put it into a saucepan with 1 tbsp water. Cook gently for 2-3 minutes. Leave to cool, then mix the apple into the yogurt and mash with a fork.

4 **C** ½ 🥛 ½ 🐟 1½ 🥚
banana and peach smoothie

makes **2** portions
¼ ripe small banana
1 small peach, stone removed
100ml breast milk or formula milk

Peel and chop the banana and peach. Mix with the breast milk or formula milk and whiz with a hand-held blender (or in a food processor or blender) until smooth.

4 **C** ½ 🥛 ½ 🐟 1½ 🥚
mango lassi

makes **2** portions
1 small mango
5 tbsp natural full-fat yogurt

Cut through the mango on either side of the fruit's stone. Peel off the skin and then cut the mango flesh into cubes. Put the mango into a bowl. Add the yogurt and whiz with a hand-held blender (or in a food processor or blender) until smooth.

½ 🥛 ½ 🐟 1½ 🥚
banana and fig yogurt

makes **2** portions
1 small ripe banana
1 fresh fig
3 tbsp natural full-fat yogurt

Peel and chop the banana, then put it in a bowl. Wash, stalk and finely chop the fig. Mash the banana, add the fig, mash again, then stir into the yogurt. This recipe is only suitable for babies who are confident with chewing.

2 **C** 1 🐟 1½ 🍃 4 🥚
fruity muesli

50g ground baby muesli
1 ripe apricot
50ml apple juice

Put the muesli into a bowl. Cut the apricot in half, remove the stone and chop the flesh. Put the fruit into a bowl and purée with a hand-held blender. Add to the ground muesli with the apple juice and mix together. Remember, do no serve muesli containing nuts if there is any family history of allergies.

1 slice of raisin bread (only for
9-month-old babies plus)
100ml breast milk or formula milk
1 ripe pear

raisin bread soaked in milk with banana

Tear the raisin bread into small pieces and put it in a bowl. Pour over the breast milk or formula milk and leave to soak for 5–10 minutes. Peel and core the pear and finely chop the flesh. Stir through the softened bread. Mash with a fork.

Vitamin B₁

1 Weetabix
100ml breast milk or formula milk
1 small ripe banana

weetabix with banana

Break the Weetabix into small pieces and put in a bowl. Add the breast milk or formula milk. Peel and mash the banana, then mix all the ingredients together and serve. This is only suitable for babies who are confident with chewing.

 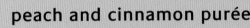

makes **2 portions**
100g couscous
50ml apple juice
3 fresh apricots

apricot couscous

Put the couscous in a bowl and pour over the apple juice and 50ml boiling water. Cover and leave for 10 minutes. Remove the stones from the apricots and peel (optional), then roughly mash. Fluff the couscous with a fork and mix with the mashed apricots. This is only suitable for babies who are confident with chewing.

1 ripe peach
1 pinch of ground cinnamon

peach and cinnamon purée

Stone and peel the peach, then mash the flesh in a bowl until smooth. Add a pinch of ground cinnamon and mix well.

soft bread

1 slice of white bread
2 tbsp natural full-fat yogurt
2 tbsp breast milk or formula milk

Tear the bread into small pieces and put it into a bowl. Add the yogurt and breast milk or formula milk and then leave for 5–10 minutes to soften. This recipe is only suitable for babies who are confident with chewing.

makes **2 portions**
1 ripe medium papaya
3 tbsp baby rice
3 tbsp breast milk or formula milk

papaya and rice

Cut the papaya in half, remove the seeds and then peel. Finely chop the flesh of the fruit and then put it into a bowl. Mix together the baby rice and breast milk or formula milk. Add to the papaya and whiz with a hand-held blender (or in a food processor or blender).

¼ ripe melon, eg Ogen
75g fresh blueberries

melon and mashed blueberries

Peel the melon and finely chop it. Put the fresh blueberries into a bowl, mash roughly, and mix with the melon.

All quick bites make 1 portion
unless otherwise stated.

breakfasts to freeze

buttermilk and nut scones

makes: 20 baby portions

storage: up to 2 months in the freezer

450g self-raising flour
pinch of ground cinnamon
60g unsalted butter
2 tbsp finely ground nuts
  (optional)
284ml buttermilk
6 tbsp breast milk or
  formula milk

These little scones are quick to make and freeze brilliantly. Serve them soaked in a little formula milk or soya drink to babies who are confident with chewing. For older babies they make great nibbles when teething. Remember, if there is any history of allergy, particularly nut allergy, it is best to leave the nuts out.

1 Preheat the oven to 180°C/350°F/gas mark 4. Sieve the flour and cinnamon into a large bowl. Rub in the butter, then stir in the nuts (if using) and buttermilk.
2 Add enough breast milk or formula milk to make a soft, sticky dough.
3 Drop teaspoonfuls of the mixture onto a buttered baking sheet. Bake for 12–14 minutes, until golden and cooked through.
4 Leave to cool on a wire rack, then freeze in freezer bags.
5 To serve, thaw thoroughly, break into very small pieces and soak in a little formula milk.

apricot and vanilla purée

makes: 4–5 baby portions

storage: up to 2 months in the freezer

8 ripe fresh apricots, stoned
4 tbsp water
4 tbsp fresh orange juice
1 vanilla pod

Vanilla is a fantastic ingredient for babies and children. It gives dishes a lovely, natural, sweet flavour without the addition of sugar. It also helps bring out the flavour of many soft fruits, apricots and peaches in particular. Once you have used the vanilla pod, wash it and leave it to dry on kitchen paper. You can then re-use it, or put it into a jar of golden caster sugar to use for baking.

1 Chop the apricots into small pieces and put them into a small saucepan with the water and orange juice.
2 Split the vanilla pod lengthways and add to the pan. Heat gently until just simmering, and cook until the apricots are soft (approximately 10 minutes).
3 Remove from the heat and cool. Remove the vanilla pod before whizzing the fruit with a hand-held blender (or in a food processor or blender) until smooth.
4 Spoon the purée into ice-cube trays. Cover with foil or put into a freezer bag and seal. Freeze.
5 To serve, thaw thoroughly.

Note: not all recipes in this section are suitable for all babies in the age group. Please read the recipe introductions carefully before serving them to your baby.

oatcakes

makes: 10 baby portions

storage: up to 3 months in the freezer

125ml boiling water
1 tsp unsalted butter
150g fresh medium oatmeal

A great stand-by, these are quick to make and older babies who are confident with chewing love them. Your baby shouldn't have too much butter in his or her diet, and always make sure it is unsalted. In fact, it's a good opportunity to change to unsalted butter for all the family. Only serve these to babies who are confident with chewing.

1 Preheat the oven to 180°C/350°F/gas mark 4.
2 Put the boiling water into a bowl and stir in the butter until it has melted. Stir in the oatmeal and leave to stand for 5 minutes.
3 Turn the dough out onto a floured surface and roll out to 0.5cm thick. Using a sharp knife, cut into small 2.5cm squares.
4 Put the oatcakes onto a lightly greased baking sheet and then cook for 8–10 minutes, or until just turning brown. Cool and layer between greaseproof paper in a freezer-proof container.
5 To serve, thaw thoroughly and break into very small pieces.

raspberry and blueberry compote

makes: 3–4 baby portions

storage: up to 2 months in the freezer

200g raspberries, fresh or frozen
200g fresh blueberries
6 tbsp water

Always pick over soft fruit for leaves and bugs – the easiest way to do this is to lay them on something white, such as kitchen paper. In the autumn, look out for bilberries, a type of blueberry which has a distinctive bright-blue juice and a delicious flavour.

1 Put the raspberries and blueberries into a small saucepan with the water. Heat gently until just simmering and cook until all the fruit has burst and the raspberries are pulpy.
2 Remove from the heat and cool before whizzing with a hand-held blender (or in a food processor or blender).
3 Spoon the purée into ice-cube trays. Cover with foil or put into a freezer bag and seal. Freeze.
4 To serve, thaw thoroughly.

pear and apple muffins

½

Vitamin B₁₂

makes: 16 baby portions

storage: for up to 2 months in the freezer

185g plain flour
1 tsp baking powder
1 tsp bicarbonate of soda
80g golden caster sugar
1 large free-range egg
125ml breast milk or formula milk
3 tbsp unsalted butter, melted
150g mixed pear and apple, peeled and finely chopped

Try making these in mini-muffin cases, which will help to keep the muffins fresher and more moist for longer. Muffins are always popular with babies, especially when they are beginning to teethe – but only serve them to babies who are confident with chewing. The fruits can be substituted with almost any other soft fruit.

1 Preheat the oven to 200°C/400°F/gas mark 6.
2 Butter the mini-muffin tins.
3 Sift the flour, baking powder and bicarbonate of soda into a bowl.
4 Make a well in the centre. Add the remaining ingredients, gently folding everything together to make a wet batter.
5 Spoon the batter into the buttered tins. Bake for about 12 minutes, or until the muffins are golden brown and firm to the touch.
6 Cool on a wire rack, then freeze in freezer bags.
7 To serve, thaw thoroughly and break into very small pieces.

apple and dried apricot purée

½

makes: 3 baby portions

storage: for up to 2 months in the freezer

6 dried apricots (only for 9-month-old babies plus)
100ml boiling water
4 eating apples, eg Cox's orange pippin

Dried fruits can be difficult to digest, so I'd advise keeping this one for 9-month-old babies plus plus. Make this purée in the autumn, when apples are plentiful and cheap; look out for different varieties.

1 Roughly chop the apricots and then put them into a bowl. Pour over the boiling water. Leave to soak for at least an hour, but preferably overnight. (The longer you soak the apricots, the more water they will absorb.)
2 Peel and core the apples, then cut into small chunks. Put into a small saucepan with the soaked apricots and, if the fruit looks dry, a little extra water. Bring to simmering point and cook gently until the apples are soft and pulpy.
3 Remove from the heat and cool before whizzing with a hand-held blender (or in a food processor or blender).
4 Spoon the purée into ice-cube trays. Cover with foil or put into a freezer bag and seal. Freeze.
5 To serve, thaw thoroughly.

fresh savouries

fruity moroccan chicken

14

1½

1

½

2

Vitamin B₁, A

1+

makes: 4 baby portions or 2 baby portions and 1 adult portion

storage: up to 24 hours in the refrigerator

1 tbsp olive oil
1 large onion, peeled and
chopped
1 clove garlic, peeled and
finely chopped
450g raw chicken, finely
chopped
100g dried apricots, finely
chopped and 75g sultanas
(only for 9-month-old
babies plus)
pinch of ground cinnamon
400ml tomato passata
200ml water
couscous, to serve

The classic Moroccan combination of fruit, meat, and mild spices is always popular with babies. You could make this with lamb or beef mince instead of chicken – just change the cooking time accordingly. Serve with couscous. Non-organic dried fruits are treated with the preservative sulphur dioxide, which may provoke allergic reactions, so buy organic when possible. This is only suitable for 9-month-old babies plus, who are confident with chewing.

1 Heat the oil in a small frying pan and fry the onion and garlic until soft and pale golden.
2 Add the chicken and fry, stirring often, until browned.
3 Add the apricots, sultanas, cinnamon, tomato passata and water.
4 Bring the mixture to the boil, then reduce the heat and simmer gently for 20 minutes.
5 Meanwhile, cook the couscous for the length of time that is specified on the packet.
6 Serve the chicken mixture mashed if necessary with couscous or finely chopped rice or pasta.

baked potato with two cheeses

10½

½

1½

2

1

1+

makes: 1 baby portion

storage: best eaten immediately

1 medium potato
25g Cheddar cheese, grated
3 tbsp cottage cheese,

Note: not all recipes in this section are suitable for all babies in the age group. Please read the introductions carefully before serving

Don't waste time and energy by cooking just one baked potato – cook a few. Have one for lunch and use the flesh from the others to make a purée that can be frozen and reheated. You could use a sweet potato for this recipe instead.

1 Preheat the oven to 180°C/350°F/gas mark 4. Wash the potato and stick it on a metal skewer or cut a cross in the top.
2 Cook for 1 hour, or until the potato is cooked through. Meanwhile sieve the cottage cheese. Allow the potato to cool slightly, and then cut in half and scoop out the flesh. Mash the potato with the cheeses and purée if necessary.

chicken with sesame seeds

 14

 2

 2

 1

makes: 2 baby portions or 1 baby portion and 1 small adult portion

storage: best eaten immediately

1 raw chicken breast

1 small head broccoli, cut into small florets

1 tbsp olive oil

2 tsp sesame seeds, ground

4

 1+

If you have the time, toast the sesame seeds to give them a more pronounced nutty flavour. You could also add a dash of sesame oil to the olive oil. This recipe makes enough for lunch for an adult as well; if you don't fancy eating it, just quarter the recipe. Do not feed seeds to babies if there is any family history of allergies.

1 Cut the chicken into thin strips.
2 Bring a pan of water to the boil and cook the broccoli until just soft (approximately 3-4 minutes).
3 Heat the oil in a pan and fry the chicken until golden. Add the cooked broccoli and sesame seeds and cook for 5 more minutes, until the chicken is cooked through.
4 Chop the chicken and broccoli into small pieces and mash.

tomato and aubergine beef

10

1

3

1 C

Vitamin B$_{12}$

 1+

makes: 8 baby portions or 2 baby portions and 3 adult portions

storage: up to 3 days in the refrigerator

2 tbsp olive oil

500g beef mince

1 onion, peeled and finely chopped

1 clove garlic, peeled and finely chopped

1 small aubergine, chopped into small dice

400g fresh vine tomatoes or 400g tin chopped tomatoes

200ml no-salt vegetable stock

1 tbsp tomato purée

1 tbsp chopped fresh mixed herbs or just parsley (or pinch dried herbs)

tiny pasta or rice, to serve

I am not a fan of baby books that encourage you to make mince dishes with just 100g of meat. If you are going to cook mince, you may as well make it worth your while and do enough to feed the whole family. Adding aubergine to the mince is a great way of making it go further, but it also gives it a lovely rich flavour.

1 Heat a frying pan until really hot. Add 1 tbsp of the olive oil and fry the beef until it is really brown all over (approximately 5–10 minutes). Transfer the meat to a plate.
2 Heat the remaining oil in the pan and fry the onion, garlic, and aubergine until they are soft and golden, stirring often.
3 Return the beef to the pan and add the tomatoes, vegetable stock, tomato purée and dried herbs (if using), then cover and simmer for 25 minutes.
4 Meanwhile, bring a large pan of water to the boil and cook the pasta according to the packet's instructions.
5 Add the fresh herbs to the sauce, cook for a further 1-2 minutes, then mash. Spoon the sauce over the pasta, or purée a small amount of each together in a small bowl.

butterbean and carrot pâté

2½

1

½

1

Vitamin A

1+

makes: 3 baby portions or
1 baby and 1 adult portion

storage: up to 24 hours in the refrigerator

200g carrots, peeled and
  chopped
2 tbsp olive oil
200g tin butterbeans
pinch of paprika
1 tsp chopped coriander
  (optional)
toast, to serve (optional)

As your baby gets older and increasingly used to solids, you can start to introduce more fibrous foods – as long as they are well-cooked and puréed. Beans and pulses are an excellent source of many nutrients, but especially protein, and so are ideal for vegetarian babies. Canned beans are fine, although some can have high levels of salt, so check the labels and make sure you rinse them well before use.

1 Put a pan of water on to boil and cook the carrots in a steamer over the pan, until they are soft (about 4 minutes).

2 Put the carrots and all the other ingredients into a blender (or food processor) and whiz until smooth.

3 If your baby is confident with chewing, spread the pate on to toast and cut it into fingers.

minestrone

5½

1

1

1

1½

Vitamin B₁, A

1+

makes: 3 baby portions or
1 baby portion and 1 adult portion

storage: up to 3 days in the refrigerator

1 tbsp olive oil
2 spring onions, finely
  chopped
1 small carrot, peeled and
  diced
½ leek, washed and finely
  chopped
200g tin chopped tomatoes
300ml vegetable stock
100g tiny pasta shapes
1 tbsp freshly grated cheese,
  eg Parmesan

When using vegetable stock, make sure it is a no-salt brand because too much salt can be dangerous for small babies. If you can't find a brand without salt, just use water. Many varieties of tinned tomatoes often have added sugar and salt, so you should always check the labels and look for ones without these unnecessary ingredients.

1 Heat the olive oil in a large pan. Add the spring onions, carrot, and leek and cook until the vegetables are soft and the spring onions are just golden.

2 Add the tomatoes and vegetable stock and bring to the boil. Simmer for 15–20 minutes, until the vegetables are tender.

3 Add the pasta and cook following the packet's instructions, stirring often.

4 Stir in the grated cheese and purée.

pea and cheese omelette

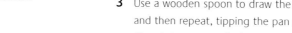

makes: 2 baby portions or 1 baby portion and 1 small adult portion

storage: best eaten immediately

3 medium free-range eggs

freshly ground black pepper

1 tbsp grated cheese, eg Cheddar or Parmesan

small knob of unsalted butter

50g frozen petits pois or peas, cooked

Vitamin B₁, B₁, A

Often parents worry about giving babies food that is too strongly flavoured, so their diets are frequently bland. Most mass-produced mild Cheddar cheese really has no discernable flavour; you don't need to go to the extremes and give them extra-mature, but just choose something with a little more bite. This recipe is only suitable for babies who are confident with chewing.

1 Break the eggs into a bowl. Season with a little ground black pepper to taste and very lightly beat. Add the grated cheese.

2 Melt the butter in a heavy-based frying pan – or better still, an omelette pan – over a medium heat and then pour in the eggs. Turn up the heat and tilt the pan so that the eggs completely cover the base. Sprinkle the peas over the top of the omelette.

3 Use a wooden spoon to draw the egg mixture from the sides into the middle and then repeat, tipping the pan at the same time until the eggs are cooked. Chop into very small pieces.

bubble and squeak with cheese

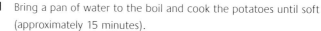

makes: 4 baby portions or 1 baby portion and 1 large adult portions

storage: best eaten immediately

500g potatoes, peeled and cut into small dice

100g Savoy cabbage, finely shredded

50g grated Cheddar cheese

½ tsp grainy mustard

small knob of unsalted butter

Vitamin B₁

A classic dish, usually made with leftovers. In fact leftovers, especially from Sunday roasts, often make perfect baby foods because cooked vegetables are quickly and easily reheated. You could make this with cabbage and any cold root vegetables, such as potatoes, parsnips or carrots.

1 Bring a pan of water to the boil and cook the potatoes until soft (approximately 15 minutes).

2 Meanwhile, steam the cabbage over the top of the boiling pan for 5-6 minutes, until tender.

3 When the vegetables are done, drain them and put into a large bowl. Add the grated cheese and the mustard. Mash with a potato masher.

4 Heat the butter in a large, heavy-based pan and add the "bubble and squeak". Cook over a medium heat and, using a spatula, carefully turn over when the bottom becomes golden.

5 Mash a little more or purée with a hand-held blender (or in a food processor or blender).

poached fish with spinach sauce

makes: 2 baby portions or 1 baby portion and 1 small adult portion

storage: best eaten immediately

12½

1

1

3

1 C

Vitamin B₁₂ A

1+

25g unsalted butter

25g plain flour

200ml breast milk, formula milk or calcium-enriched soya drink

50g Cheddar cheese, grated

100g fresh spinach, cooked and finely chopped

tiny pinch of grated nutmeg

200g white fish, skinned and boned

Try making this with tinned fish, such as tuna or salmon, if time is short. Otherwise, a good idea is to buy some fish from your fishmonger and get him to fillet it and cut it into manageable pieces. You can then check it carefully for bones before wrapping the pieces individually and freezing them. This is a great freezer stand-by because the fish thaws quickly and can be easily poached for a fast meal.

1 To make the sauce, melt the butter in a pan and add the flour. Cook for 1 minute, stirring constantly.
2 Off the heat, gradually add the milk, stirring frequently, until the sauce is smooth. Return the pan to the heat and cook until the sauce thickens. Cool slightly and stir in the cheese, chopped spinach and nutmeg.
3 Put the fish in a small pan. Cover with milk or water and poach for 5 minutes, until the flesh is just opaque. Lift the fish out carefully with a slotted spoon and serve with the sauce. Mash or purée.

lamb with butternut squash

makes: 3 baby portions or 1 baby portion and 1 adult portion

storage: up to 24 hours in the refrigerator

8

1

2

1 C

Vitamin B₁₂, B₁, A

1+

1 tbsp olive oil

200g lamb mince

small knob of unsalted butter

1 medium red onion, peeled and finely chopped

1 small clove garlic, peeled and crushed

200g butternut squash flesh, peeled and cut into small dice

tiny pinch of grated nutmeg or ground ginger (optional)

100ml no-salt vegetable stock or water

In late summer and autumn there are lots of different squashes available, so experiment with different types. Butternut is one of the sweetest and creamiest. If you have herbs growing in your garden, try adding a little thyme, sage or rosemary. Serve with a little couscous.

1 Heat the oil in a heavy-based pan and fry the lamb, breaking it up with a spoon, until golden brown. Tip onto a plate and reserve.
2 Add the butter to the pan, and when it is bubbling, add the onions and garlic. Fry until just soft, add the squash and nutmeg or ginger, and cook for a further 5 minutes, stirring often.
3 Return the mince to the pan, add the stock, and simmer gently for 15–20 minutes, until the squash is soft and the lamb is tender.
4 Finely chop into tiny pieces. Alternatively, for a smoother purée, whiz with a hand-held blender (or in a food processor or blender).

quick bites savouries

3 2½ ½ 2 9

tomato and mozzarella couscous

50g couscous
1 ripe tomato
2 slices mozzarella cheese
(approximately 40g)

Put the couscous into a bowl and add 50ml of boiling water. Cover and leave for at least 10 minutes. Fluff the couscous with a fork. Finely chop the tomato and mozzarella cheese, then add to the couscous. Mix all of the ingredients together and then mash them slightly with either a fork or a potato masher.

3 ½ ½ 2

potato salad

2 new potatoes
2 fresh mint leaves
2 tbsp natural full-fat yogurt
1 tsp lemon juice

Peel the potatoes and put them into a saucepan with a little water. Bring to the boil and simmer until just tender (approximately 7-10 minutes), then drain. Chop the potatoes into small pieces and finely chop the mint leaves. Mix together the yogurt, lemon juice and mint in a bowl. Add the potatoes and toss all the ingredients together. Mash the mixture with either a fork or a potato masher.

 3 ½ ½ 1
Vitamin B₁

guacamole

1 avocado (of which you
will use ½)
2 fresh coriander leaves
1 small ripe tomato (optional)
a little baby rice, to serve

Peel and halve the avocado, leaving the stone in the half you are not using in order to delay browning. Finely chop the coriander and tomato. Mash the flesh of the avocado half with the coriander. Add the tomato if your baby is confident with chewing. Serve with a little baby rice mixed with breast or formula milk.

2½ 2½ ½ 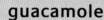 1½ 1

avocado and cheese tortillas

1 avocado (of which you will use ½)
1 flour tortilla
25g mild or medium Cheddar
cheese

Peel and halve the avocado, leaving the stone in the half you are not using in order to delay browning. Mash the avocado, then spread it onto a flour tortilla. Grate the cheese and sprinkle it over the avocado. Roll up the tortilla and cut into small circles. This is only suitable for babies who are confident with chewing.

 3 ½ 1 2
Vitamin B₁

courgette and mint purée

1 small courgette
5 green beans
handful of fresh or frozen peas
2 fresh mint leaves

Finely chop the courgette and put into a steamer or saucepan with the green beans, peas, and mint leaves. Cook for 5 minutes, or until just tender. Drain and whiz with a hand-held blender (or in a food processor or blender). Serve with little fingers of soft bread or roll if your baby is confident with chewing.

Vitamin B₁, A   ½   ½   ½   6

2 fish fingers
2 small carrots

fish fingers with puréed carrot

Grill the fish fingers following the pack's instructions, then cut them into small pieces. Peel and chop the carrots, then put them into a pan with a little water and bring to the boil. Simmer until tender (approximately 4-5 minutes). Drain and purée with a hand-held blender or potato masher. Serve the fish fingers with the carrot purée. This is only suitable for babies who are confident with chewing.

2 **C**   1   1   ½   3½

1 small ripe tomato
3 tbsp hummus
2 tbsp full-fat or natural yogurt
pitta fingers, to serve

hummus and tomato with pitta

Finely chop the tomato. Put the hummus (which can be bought or home-made) into a bowl, and add the yogurt and tomato. Mix together well. Serve with little pitta fingers. This is only suitable for babies who are confident with chewing.

Vitamin B₁, A   4 **C**   1   ½   3½

1 medium potato
1 small carrot
handful of fresh or frozen sweetcorn

potato purée with sweetcorn and carrot

Peel and roughly chop the potato and carrot. Put the potato into a saucepan with a little water, bring to the boil and simmer for 5 minutes. Add the carrot and sweetcorn. Continue to cook for another 5 minutes, until all the vegetables are just tender. Drain and purée with a hand-held blender or potato masher.

Vitamin B₁₂   2 **C**   ½   ½   8

2 chestnut mushrooms, cleaned
knob of butter
50g tinned tuna
1 small ripe tomato
piece fresh bread (optional)

mushrooms with tuna

Finely chop the mushrooms. Heat the butter in small frying pan and sauté the mushrooms until they are really soft. Add the tinned tuna. Finely chop the tomato and mix into the other ingredients. Lightly mash with a fork. Serve on its own or, if your baby is confident with chewing, with pieces of fresh bread.

Vitamin B₁₂   ½   3   ½   9½

2 slices cooked lamb
2 tbsp full-fat natural yogurt
2 fresh mint leaves
1 pitta bread (optional)

lamb with mint and yogurt

Finely chop the cooked lamb and mix with the yogurt. Finely chop the mint and mix into the dish. Lightly mash with a potato masher or fork. Serve with a portion of sweet potato purée and onion (see page 62).

Vitamin B₁   ½ **C** 1½   ½   12½

1 avocado (of which you will use ½)
½ small cooked chicken breast
2 fingers of fresh bread

avocado with chopped cooked chicken

Peel and halve the avocado, leaving the stone in the half you are not using in order to delay browning. Mash the avocado and finely chop the cooked chicken breast, then mix the two together. Serve with a couple of fingers of fresh bread. This recipe is only suitable for babies who are confident with chewing.

All quick bites make 1 portion unless otherwise stated.

savouries **to freeze**

salmon, broccoli and pasta

makes: 6 baby portions

storage: for up to 2 months in the freezer

100g tiny pasta shapes
200g broccoli, cut into small
  florets
200ml formula milk or
  calcium-enriched soya drink
20g plain flour
20g unsalted butter
freshly ground black pepper
100g Cheddar cheese, grated
200g cooked salmon, cut
  into small chunks

Vitamin B₁, B₁₂, A

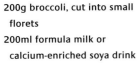
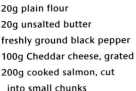

This is the sort of food I grew up on. Cool the sauce before adding the other ingredients and then freeze, so that the cooked fish is only reheated once.

1 Bring a pan of water to the boil and cook the pasta following the packet's instructions. Cook the broccoli over the boiling pasta water in a steamer, until just tender (approximately 5 minutes). Drain and reserve.

2 Preheat the oven to 180°C/350°F/gas mark 4.

3 Mix together the milk, flour, and butter in a saucepan. Heat gently, stirring constantly with a whisk, until you have a smooth sauce.

4 Season with pepper, add half the cheese, and stir until melted, then stir in the cooked pasta. Stir in the salmon and broccoli and pour into an ovenproof dish. Sprinkle with remaining cheese. Bake for 25 minutes, until golden. Cool and freeze.

5 To serve, thaw thoroughly and bake at 180°C/350°F/gas mark 4 for 15-20 minutes, or until hot through, and then chop into tiny pieces.

macaroni and cauliflower cheese

makes: 4–6 baby portions

storage: up to 2 months in the freezer

100g macaroni
400g cauliflower florets
200ml formula milk
20g plain flour
20g unsalted butter
freshly ground black pepper
2 tbsp finely chopped parsley
100g Cheddar cheese, grated

Vitamin B₁, B₁₂

Note: not all recipes in this section are suitable for all babies in the age group. Please read the introductions carefully before serving

Keep some of the tiny tender cauliflower leaves to steam with the florets and add to the dish for extra vitamins if your baby is confident with chewing.

1 Bring a pan of water to the boil and cook the macaroni following the packet's instructions. Cook the cauliflower over the boiling water in a steamer, until just tender (approximately 5 minutes). Drain and reserve.

2 Preheat the oven to 180°C/350°F/gas mark 4.

3 Mix together the milk, flour, and butter in a pan. Heat gently, stirring with a whisk, until you have a smooth sauce. Season with pepper, then add the herbs and half the cheese. Stir until the cheese has melted, then stir in the macaroni.

4 Arrange the cauliflower in an ovenproof dish. Pour over the macaroni cheese and sprinkle over the remaining cheese. Bake for 15 minutes until golden brown.

5 Leave to cool completely wrap in foil and freeze.

6 To serve, thaw thoroughly and bake at 180°C/350°F/gas mark 4 for 15-20 minutes, or until hot through, and then chop into tiny pieces or mash.

sweet potato and coconut curry

makes: 10 baby portions

storage: up to 2 months in the freezer

1½

½

½

2½

Vitamin A

25g unsalted butter

1 tbsp olive oil

1 onion, peeled, chopped

1 garlic clove, peeled, crushed

1–2 tsp mild curry powder

1cm fresh root ginger, peeled and finely chopped

1 small butternut squash, peeled and the flesh cut into small dice

1 small sweet potato, peeled and cut into small dice

1 carrot, cut into small dice

200g tin chopped tomatoes

400ml coconut milk

300ml no-salt vegetable stock

Older babies and children enjoy a creamy, coconut curry – in fact, having Thai curry is a great treat for Ella, my eldest. Try adding a little lime juice to give it a bit of a kick. This recipe is designed to feed the whole family, but if you only want enough for a few meals for the baby just halve the recipe. Do not feed coconut to babies if there is any family history of allergies.

1 Heat the butter and oil in a large pan, add the onion and garlic and cook until soft (approximately 5 minutes).

2 Add 1 tsp curry powder and ginger and cook for 1 more minute, stirring the mixture often. Add the butternut squash, sweet potato and carrot and then cook for 2 minutes, stirring.

3 Add the tomatoes, coconut milk, and stock and bring to the boil. Simmer for 15–20 minutes, until the vegetables are just tender.

4 Leave to cool completely, then spoon into a freezer-proof container. Freeze.

5 To serve, thaw thoroughly. Put into a saucepan and heat through for 10-15 minutes, or until hot through. Lightly mash or, for a smoother purée, whiz with a hand-held blender (or in a food processor or blender).

creamy tomato soup

makes: 10 baby portions

storage: up to 2 months in the freezer

½

½

1

1

Vitamin A

10g unsalted butter

1 small red onion, peeled and finely chopped

1 small garlic clove, peeled and crushed

1 small carrot, peeled and finely chopped

1 small potato, peeled and diced

500g ripe tomatoes, chopped

1 tbsp tomato purée

600ml no-salt vegetable stock

a few torn basil leaves

50g full-fat cream cheese or 50ml formula milk

This soup is absolutely delicious and freezes brilliantly. The quantities are easily doubled if you are feeding a family.

1 Heat the butter in a large saucepan. Add the onion, garlic and carrot and cook until soft and golden (about 5 minutes). Add the potato and cook for another 5 minutes.

2 Add the tomatoes, tomato purée, stock and basil. Stir and bring to the boil, then simmer for 8–10 minutes, until the potatoes are soft.

3 Whiz with a hand-held blender (or in a food processor or blender) until smooth, then pass through a nylon sieve.

4 Leave to cool. Pour into a freezer-proof container and freeze.

5 To serve, thaw thoroughly. Stir in the cream cheese or milk and reheat gently.

sweetcorn and potato soup

makes: 10 baby portions

storage: up to 2 months in the freezer

1 tbsp olive oil

2 unsmoked streaky bacon rashers, finely chopped

10g unsalted butter

1 small onion, peeled and finely chopped

1 small garlic clove, peeled and crushed

1 medium potato, peeled and cut into small dice

250g tin sweetcorn, drained

1 tbsp parsley, finely chopped

175ml no-salt vegetable stock

125ml formula milk or calcium-enriched soya drink

If you make this soup in the summer, use a couple of new potatoes instead of a single large potato and just scrub them well instead of peeling. This will increase the fibre content of this dish, which is fine for babies that are used to solids. Also, because most of the nutrients in potatoes are stored just under the skin, they will be retained.

1 Heat the oil in a large pan and fry the bacon until crisp and golden. Reserve on a plate.

2 Add the butter to the pan and use it to fry the onion and garlic until soft and pale golden (approximately 5 minutes). Add the potato and cook for a further 5 minutes, stirring often. Add the sweetcorn, cooked bacon, and fresh parsley and stir well.

3 Pour in the stock, bring to the boil, then simmer gently for 15 minutes.

4 Whiz with a hand-held blender (or in a food processor or blender) until smooth, then pass through a nylon sieve.

5 Leave to cool. Pour in a freezerproof container and freeze.

6 To serve, thaw thoroughly. Add the milk and reheat gently before serving.

creamy mushroom pasta sauce

makes: 6 baby portions

storage: up to 2 months in the freezer

1 tbsp olive oil

3 spring onions, finely chopped

300g mushrooms, sliced

1 tbsp fresh parsley, finely chopped

freshly ground black pepper

100ml no-salt vegetable stock

50g full-fat cream cheese

baby pasta or rice, cooked

Mushrooms are perennially popular with babies and young children. They shouldn't be washed because they soak up water easily – it's best to gently wipe them well with some damp kitchen paper. Try using brown cap mushrooms because they have more flavour than ordinary button mushrooms.

1 Heat the oil in a large frying pan, add the spring onions and cook until soft and translucent (approximately 5 minutes).

2 Add the mushrooms and fry until they are golden and just beginning to lose their liquid. Add the parsley and black pepper and stir well. Pour in the stock and cook over a gentle heat until the mushrooms are soft (about 4 minutes).

3 Stir in the cream cheese. Spoon into a freezer-proof container and freeze.

4 To serve, thaw thoroughly. Whiz with a hand-held blender (or in a food processor or blender) until smooth, then pour over cooked baby pasta or rice.

ratatouille

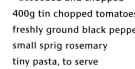

Vitamin A

makes: 6–8 baby portions

storage: up to 2 months in the freezer

2 small aubergines
2 courgettes
2 tbsp olive oil
1 medium red onion, peeled and chopped
1 small garlic clove, peeled and crushed
2 small red peppers, deseeded and chopped
400g tin chopped tomatoes
freshly ground black pepper
small sprig rosemary
tiny pasta, to serve

Another versatile dish that can be served with baked potatoes, pasta or rice. You could also use it as the base for a vegetarian lasagne.

1 Cut the aubergines and courgettes into small chunks
2 Heat the oil in a heavy-based pan and fry the onion until soft and golden (approximately 5 minutes). Add the garlic and aubergines and fry until soft, adding a little more oil if necessary.
3 Add the red peppers and courgettes and cook over a low heat for 25 minutes.
4 Add the tomatoes, black pepper and rosemary. Cover the pan with a lid and cook for another 20 minutes, stirring occasionally.
5 Leave to cool. Spoon into a freezerproof container and freeze.
6 To serve, thaw thoroughly. Put into a saucepan and heat through for 10-15 minutes, or until hot through. Remove the rosemary stalk, the chop the ratatouille finely or whiz with a hand-held blender (or in a food processor or blender) until smooth, then pour over cooked baby pasta.

herby tomato pasta sauce

makes: 6 baby portions

storage: up to 2 months in the freezer

1 tbsp olive oil
1 small onion, peeled and finely chopped
1 small garlic clove, peeled and crushed
4 fresh plum tomatoes, chopped
200g tin chopped tomatoes
2 basil leaves
freshly ground black pepper (optional)
2 tbsp fresh herbs, eg thyme, sage, parsley, rosemary, finely chopped
tiny baby pasta, to serve

This is a great freezer stand-by and can be served with noodles, rice, polenta, or even just plain old mashed potato. To make it a bit more substantial, after defrosting, try adding a small tin of flaked tuna or shredded cooked chicken and heat through thoroughly.

1 Heat the oil in a heavy-based saucepan and fry the onion until soft and pale golden (approximately 5 minutes). Add the garlic and cook for 1 more minute.
2 Add the fresh and tinned tomatoes and basil, black pepper (if using), and herbs and simmer for 10 minutes.
3 Whiz with a hand-held blender (or in a food processor or blender) until smooth, then pass through a nylon sieve. Leave to cool, then pour into a freezer-proof container and freeze.
4 To serve, thaw thoroughly, reheat gently, and serve over cooked baby pasta.

quick pizzas

makes: 4 baby portions

storage: up to 2 months in the freezer

200g self-raising flour

100ml fomula milk or calcium-enriched soya drink

50ml olive oil

4 tbsp tomato passata

2 medium mushrooms, finely sliced

1 slice ham, finely chopped

50g Cheddar cheese, grated

3½

½

½

1

1+

Pizzas are brilliant freezer food, but they are only suitable for babies who are confident with chewing.

1 Preheat the oven to 180°C/350°F/gas mark 4.

2 Sift the flour into a bowl and make a well in the centre. Pour in the milk and olive oil and, using a fork, draw the mixture together to form a dough.

3 Tip the dough out onto a floured surface and divide into four. Roll each chunk into a ball and, using a rolling pin, press it out flat on a lightly greased baking sheet.

4 Spread 1 tbsp tomato passata on each circle and top with the mushrooms and ham.

5 Sprinkle a little cheese over each one and bake for 5-10 minutes. Leave to cool. Individually wrap in foil and freeze.

6 To serve, thaw thoroughly and bake at 180°C/350°F/gas mark 4 for 5-10 minutes. Chop into very small pieces.

mini shepherd's pies

makes: 12 baby portions

storage: up to 3 months in the freezer

7½

1

2

1

Vitamin B₁,B₁₂, A

1+

2 tbsp olive oil

600g lamb mince

1 medium leek, chopped

2 medium carrots, peeled and diced

1 garlic clove, peeled and crushed

100g mushrooms, sliced

200g tinned red kidney beans, rinsed and drained

400g tin chopped tomatoes

2 tbsp fresh parsley, finely chopped

400ml water

1kg potatoes, peeled, halved

freshly ground black pepper

3–4 tbsp formula milk or calcium-enriched soya drink, plus extra for glazing

knob of unsalted butter

It's more economical to make lots of a dish and freeze it instead of faffing about with tiny amounts. You can also make just the sauce and serve it with mashed potato, pasta or rice. If the texture of the shepherd's pie is too lumpy for your baby, just spoon some onto a plate and mash with a fork.

1 Heat 1 tbsp of the oil in a heavy-based pan and fry the lamb mince until browned, using a wooden spoon to break it up. Reserve on a plate.

2 Heat the remaining oil and fry the leek and carrots until soft and pale golden. Add the garlic and mushrooms and fry for another 5 minutes, stirring often.

3 Add the kidney beans, tomatoes, and herbs. Stir well. Add the water and return the mince to the pan. Season with black pepper, bring to the boil, and simmer gently for 35 minutes.

4 Meanwhile, put a pan of water on to boil and cook the potatoes until just soft (approximately 10 minutes). Drain and mash with the milk and butter.

5 Put the mince into ramekins. Top each with mashed potato. Rough the tops with a fork and brush with a little milk. Leave to cool completely, then transfer to the refrigerator when cool enough. Wrap in foil or cling film and freeze.

6 To serve, thaw thoroughly. Preheat the oven to 180°C/350°F/gas mark 4. Cook the ramekins for 20–25 minutes, until the tops are golden and crunchy and they are piping hot all the way through.

7 Lightly mash before serving if necessary.

quick bites finger foods

By this stage it is very likely that you baby will be able to move food from hand to mouth quite easily, enabling you to offer her more "finger foods". She or he will also be able to cope with foods that have more of a texture, rather than just purées, so start experimenting with a few new shapes and sizes.

1½

home-made bread sticks

makes 2 portions
2 thick slices of bread
olive oil

Cut each slice of bread into strips. Put them onto a baking sheet and drizzle with the olive oil. Bake at 180°C/350°F/gas mark 4 for 10-15 minutes, until golden, then turn them over and bake for another 10 minutes. Leave to cool, then store in an airtight container.

rice cakes

2 unsalted rice cakes

There are many types and brands of rice cakes. The most important thing is to go for a variety that has no added salt, and I'd recommend choosing an organic brand to ensure there are no GM ingredients. They are great snack for vegetarian babies and for babies on a gluten-free diet. They are delicious spread with cream cheese.

 3 C 1 ½

Vitamin A

rice cakes with mango purée

½ ripe mango
2 unsalted rice cakes

Remove the stone from the mango and peel. Cut the flesh into small pieces, put them into a bowl and mash with a fork. Spread the mango purée on the rice cakes.

2 ½ ½ ½ 2½

tomato bread

1 ciabatta loaf (of which you will use ⅛)
1 medium ripe tomato
1 fresh basil leaf
1 tbsp olive oil

Cut the ciabatta into four pieces. Slice one of the quarters in half horizontally and place this on a baking sheet. Mash the tomato in a small bowl and spread on the bread, removing the skin as you push (it should come off easily). Finely chop the basil leaf. Drizzle with the olive oil and scatter over the basil. Put under a hot grill for 2-3 minutes, then leave to cool slightly.

Vitamin B₁   3   1   4½

1 slice brown of bread
1 tbsp smooth peanut butter

peanut butter soldiers

Lightly toast the bread and spread with the peanut butter. Cut the toast into fingers. Do not serve nut products to babies if there's a family history of allergies.

Vitamin B₁₂   ½   1   1   6

1 egg
1 slice of bread, toasted

toast with boiled egg

Put an organic egg into a pan of water, bring to the boil, and simmer for 5 minutes; ensure the egg yolk is firm, with no runny bits. Peel away the shell and cut the egg into small pieces. Serve with the toast cut into soldiers.

    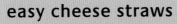

½ C   ½   ½   2

½ fruit bun (only for 9-month-old babies plus)
½ eating apple
1 slice of bread

fruit bun and apple

Cut the fruit bun half into small pieces. Peel and core the apple, then simmer in 2 tbsp water until soft. Serve the bun and the apple purée together.

   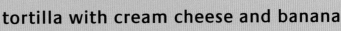

1 C   ½   ½   ½   2

makes 2 portions
1 small ripe banana
1 soft flour tortilla
1 tbsp full-fat cream cheese

tortilla with cream cheese and banana

Mash the banana. Spread the flour tortilla with the cream cheese and the mashed banana. Roll the tortilla into a long sausage and then chop into small circles, approximately 2cm in diameter.

1   ½   ½   3½

makes 8 portions
375g puff pastry
6 tbsp grated Cheddar cheese

easy cheese straws

Cut the sheet of puff pastry lengthways into eight equal strips. Sprinkle over the Cheddar cheese and press onto the pastry slightly. Carefully twist each strip to make a long, thin, twisted straw. Place the strips on a baking sheet and bake for 8-10 minutes at 180°C/350°F/gas mark 4. Leave to cool and store in an airtight container.

Vitamin B₁₂   ½   1½   ½   9½

1 egg
1 tbsp full-fat milk
tiny drop of vanilla extract (optional)
a little butter
2 slices bread

eggy bread fingers

Lightly beat the egg and place in a bowl. Add the milk and vanilla extract and mix together. Rub a little butter over the base of a frying pan and heat the pan. Dip the slices of bread into the egg mixture, making sure the bread is completely covered with egg, then put them straight into the pan. Fry gently for a couple of minutes on each side until golden. Cut into fingers and leave to cool slightly.

All of these quick bites are only suitable for babies who are confident with chewing.

All quick bites make 1 portion unless otherwise stated.

fresh **puddings**

mango and banana fool

4

1

1

1

3½ C

Vitamin B₁₂, A

1+

makes: 4 baby portions or
2 baby portions and 1 adult
portions

storage: best eaten
immediately or up to 24 hours
in the refrigerator

200ml formula milk or
   calcium-enriched soya drink
1 vanilla pod, split lengthways
3 egg yolks
1 tsp golden caster sugar
1 tbsp cornflour
1 ripe mango
1 ripe small banana, peeled
   and cut into chunks
100g natural full-fat yogurt

Calcium-enriched soya drink can be used in place of formula milk. Freeze the left-over egg whites or use them to make meringues for the rest of the family.

1 To make the custard, heat the milk with the vanilla pod in a saucepan until just below boiling point.
2 In a bowl, mix the egg yolks, caster sugar, and cornflour together, then pour the hot milk into this mixture, stirring constantly. Return the custard to the saucepan and heat it gently, stirring constantly, until the mixture thickens (approximately 10 minutes). Do not allow to boil, because it will curdle.
3 Once the custard has thickened, leave it to cool.
4 Meanwhile, cut the mango flesh on either side of the stone, then peel the fruit and cut it into chunks.
5 Put the mango into a bowl with the banana chunks and whiz together with a hand-held blender (or in a food processor or blender) until you have a smooth purée.
6 Gently fold together the cooled custard and the yogurt. Swirl through the fruit purée to make a rippled fool.

pear and almond yogurt

3

½

1

½ C

1+

makes: 2 baby portions

storage: 24 hours in the refrigerator

150g natural Greek yogurt
1 tbsp ground almonds
1 ripe pear

Note: not all recipes in this section are suitable for all babies in the age group. Please read the introductions carefully before serving

This is a delicious combination, which goes well with muesli for breakfast. Pears are one of few fruits that ripen naturally after they have been picked, so it's best to buy ones that are firm (not quite ripe) if you are not going to use them straight away. Do not feed nuts to babies if there is any family history of allergies.

1 Put the yogurt into a large bowl, add the almonds, and mix together well.
2 Cut the pear into quarters, then peel and core it.
3 Grate each quarter directly into the bowl of yogurt so you catch the juice and mix again.
4 Whiz with a hand-held blender (or in a food processor or blender) until the mixture is smooth.

rice pudding with blueberries

Vanilla gives many desserts a natural sweetness, so you really don't need to add sugar. It's best to let your baby get used to the sweet taste of fruits in desserts without extra sugar, so that she doesn't develop a sweet tooth.

1 Put the first four ingredients into a saucepan and stir.

2 Bring to the boil, then reduce the heat and simmer the rice for 15-20 minutes, stirring often to prevent the mixture from sticking on the bottom. If necessary, add a few more tablespoons of water.

3 Add the butter; mix well and cook for another minute.

4 Put the fruit into a small saucepan with 1-2 tbsp water and heat gently until the berries are just at bursting point. Mash slightly or whiz with a hand-held blender (or in a food processor or blender) until smooth.

5 Swirl the blueberries through the rice pudding before serving.

2½
½
½
1

Vitamin B₁₂

makes: 8 baby portions or 2 baby portions and 3 adult portions

storage: best eaten fresh or 24 hours in the refrigerator (but must not be reheated)

150g short-grain pudding rice
500ml formula milk or calcium-enriched soya drink
100ml water
2–3 drops vanilla extract
small knob of unsalted butter
200g blueberries

apple and raspberry custard

Home-made custard is a million miles away from the stuff made from instant custard powder. This has a subtle, delicate vanilla flavour that babies love. Don't worry about the possibility of it curdling – just don't rush!

1 To make the custard, gently heat the milk with the vanilla pod in a saucepan until just below boiling point.

2 In a bowl, mix the egg yolks, 1 tsp of the sugar, and cornflour together, then pour the hot milk over this mixture, stirring constantly. Return the custard to the saucepan and heat gently, stirring constantly, until the mixture thickens (approximately 10 minutes). Do not allow it to boil, because it will curdle.

3 Once the custard has thickened, remove the vanilla pod leave to cool.

4 Peel and core the apple, chop into small pieces and put into a saucepan with the raspberries. Add the water and the remaining sugar. Heat gently until the apple is soft and pulpy (approximately 5 minutes).

5 Mash the fruit purée or whiz with a hand-held blender (or in a food processor or blender) until smooth.

6 Serve the custard with a swirl of apple and raspberry purée.

2½
½
1
½
1

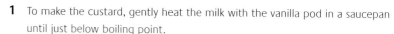
Vitamin B₁₂

makes: 4 baby portions

storage: 24 hours in the refrigerator

200ml formula milk or calcium-enriched soya drink
1 vanilla pod, split lengthways
3 medium free-range egg yolks
1½ tsp golden caster sugar
1 tbsp cornflour
1 eating apple, eg Cox's orange pippin
large handful of fresh raspberries
2 tbsp water

baked apples stuffed with fruits

2

1

½

3

1+

makes: 3 baby portions

storage: up to 24 hours in the refrigerator

4 small cooking apples, eg Bramley
100g dried fruit, eg prunes, apricots, mango, raisins (only for 9-month-old babies plus)
2 tbsp porridge oats
small knob of unsalted butter

As with potatoes, don't waste time just baking one apple – bake lots and scrape the flesh out to purée and freeze. If the apples are very tart, add a little golden caster sugar to taste; the dried fruits should add enough natural sweetness to make this quantity of sugar ample.

1 Preheat the oven to 180°C/350°F/gas mark 4.
2 Core the apples and score the skin around the middle of each apple. This will stop them from bursting in the oven. Finely chop the dried fruits and put into a bowl.
3 Add the oats and butter and mix together well.
4 Fill the cavity of each apple with the stuffing.
5 Put the apples into a lightly greased, ovenproof dish and bake for 45 minutes until the apples are tender. Scoop out the flesh and dried fruits and whiz until smooth with a hand-held blender.

summer pudding

2½

½

½

½

6

1+

makes: 4 baby portions or 2 baby portions and 2 adult portion

storage: up to 24 hours in the refrigerator

500g mixed berries, eg strawberries, raspberries, blackberries, blueberries, fresh or frozen
1 tbsp golden caster sugar
6 tbsp water
6 slices day-old white bread, crusts removed

This is easy-peasy and makes a delicious pudding for all the family. You could just as easily use a bag of frozen summer or forest fruits. This recipe is only suitable for babies who are confident with chewing.

1 Put the berries into a saucepan with the sugar and water. Bring to the boil and then simmer for 5-6 minutes, until the fruits are bursting.
2 Cut the bread in quarters into triangles. Arrange half of the triangles in the bottom of a shallow dish. Using a slotted spoon, spoon over three-quarters of the warm fruit.
3 Arrange the remaining bread triangles over the fruit and pour over the juice and remaining fruit. Press down lightly to ensure all the bread is covered with fruit juice. Leave to stand for at least an hour in a cool place before serving.
4 To serve, mash or finely chop.

quick bites puddings

   ## blueberry and pear yogurt

1 small ripe pear
small handful of blueberries
2 tbsp natural full-fat yogurt

Cut the pear into small pieces and cook in 1 tbsp water until pulpy. Put the pieces into a bowl and mash with a small handful of blueberries, then mix with the yogurt. Pears are great to give to your baby if she is constipated.

  ## fruity yogurt

2 large strawberries
2 tbsp natural full-fat yogurt

Hull and crush the strawberries until they are puréed, then mix them with the yogurt and serve.

   ## apple and carrot

2 tbsp grated eating apple
2 tbsp grated carrot

Mix together the grated apple and carrot and cook in 1 tbsp water until pulpy (approximately 4-5 minutes). Lightly mash with a hand-held blender until smooth.

    ## fruit porridge

2 dried apricots or figs and 1 tbsp raisins
(only for 9-month-old babies plus)
3 tbsp cooked porridge (page 96)

Make porridge more interesting by adding puréed dried fruit. Cook the dried fruits in 3 tbsp boiling water until soft, and then purée. Mix them with the porridge and serve.

     ## cheese and grapes

4 seedless red grapes
1 tbsp full-fat cream cheese
1 oatcake

Children love grapes. Finely chop the grapes, mix into the cream cheese and spread onto an oatcake. This is only suitable for babies who are confident with chewing.

 ## baked apples

1 eating apple
a tiny pinch of cinnamon
25g raspberries

Baking apples is an easy way to get a soft apple purée. Core your apple and score around its middle with a sharp knife. Put into a greased ovenproof dish and sprinkle with a tiny pinch of cinnamon. Bake for 20–25 minutes. Leave to cool and scoop out the flesh. Mash the raspberries with the apple flesh. (To save time bake a few apples at once and freeze the purée.)

   ## prune custard

1 tbsp prunes (only for 9-month-old babies plus)
4 tbsp custard (page 124)

Cook the prunes in a saucepan with 1 tbsp boiling water and then mash. Mix them with the warm custard.

Vitamin B₁

peach yogurt

1 ripe peach
2 tbsp natural full-fat yogurt

Peel the peach by plunging it into some boiling water for a couple of minutes and then draining it and peeling away the skin. Remove the stone and then mash the flesh well before stirring it into the natural full-fat yogurt.

iced pineapple

makes 2 portions
50g fresh pineapple

Cut the pineapple into large chunks. Freeze it for about 2-3 hours. Serve when it is semi-frozen to babies who are confident with chewing.

mango and banana smoothie

makes 2 portions
1 ripe mango
1 ripe medium banana, peeled
150ml coconut milk

Cut a mango either side of the stone and peel the flesh. Slice the banana. Put both fruits into a bowl. Add the coconut milk and whiz with a hand-held blender until smooth. Do not serve coconut if there is any family history of allergies.

   Vitamin B₁₂

strawberry lassi

makes 2 portions
1 ripe medium banana, peeled
100g strawberries
100ml natural full-fat yogurt

Slice the banana and hull and slice the strawberries. Mix the yogurt, banana, and strawberries together in a bowl. Whiz with a hand-held blender (or in a food processor or blender) until smooth.

baked banana

1 date (only for babies in their 9th month plus)
1 ripe medium banana

Finely chop the date. Leaving the skin on the banana, cut a slit into it lengthways. Stuff the banana with the date. Wrap the whole thing in kitchen foil. Bake in an oven at 190°C/375°F/gas mark 5 for 20 minutes. Leave to cool, and then lightly mash. This recipe is only suitable for babies who are confident with chewing.

baked plums

4 plums
1 tsp soft brown sugar
2 tbsp full-fat cottage cheese

Halve the plums, remove the stones, and put the fruit on a greased baking tray. Sprinkle with the sugar and roast for 20 minutes in an oven at 180°C/350°F/gas mark 4. Cool, then cut two halves into small pieces and mash with the cottage cheese. Keep the rest covered in the refrigerator for up to 48 hours.

All quick bites make 1 portion
unless otherwise stated.

puddings to freeze

blackberry and apple crumble

4

½

½

½

1½ **C**

1⁺

makes: 6 baby portions

storage: up to 3 months in the freezer

3 medium cooking apples, eg Bramley

200g blackberries

3–4 tsp golden caster sugar (or more if the fruit is tart)

4 tbsp water

for the crumble:

100g plain flour

50g unsalted butter

50g porridge oats

2 tsp golden caster sugar

pinch of ground cinnamon

A great time-saver is to make a big batch of crumble topping and then freeze it in bags ready to throw on fruits. Cooking fruit that is in season is cheap and easy. This recipe is not suitable for babies who are not confident with chewing.

1 Peel and core the apples, then cut into bite-size pieces. Put them into a pan with the blackberries, sugar and the water. Heat gently until the berries are just starting to give up their juice.

2 For the crumble, put the flour into a bowl and rub in the butter until the mixture resembles breadcrumbs. Stir in the oats, sugar and cinnamon.

3 Put the fruit in a shallow ovenproof dish or into 5 or 6 small ramekins and leave to cool, then cover and freeze. Put the crumble mix in a freezer bag and freeze.

4 To serve, thaw the fruit and crumble mixture thoroughly. You will need 4-5 tbsp crumble mix for each small ramekin. Preheat the oven to 180°C/350°F/gas mark 4. Sprinkle the crumble over the fruit and bake in the oven for 25 minutes, until the crumble is crisp and golden on top. Lightly mash if necessary.

banana fruit ice

1

½ **C**

1⁺

makes: 10 baby portions

storage: up to 2 months in the freezer

3 ripe medium bananas

1 tsp golden caster sugar

50ml formula milk

100g natural Greek yogurt

pinch of ground cinnamon

Note: not all recipes in this section are suitable for all babies in the age group. Please read the introductions carefully before serving

The easiest pudding ever! Your baby may find this mixture too cold, so just leave to soften before serving.

1 Put all the ingredients into a bowl and whiz with a hand-held blender (or whiz in a food processor or blender) until smooth.

2 Pour into a plastic tub, cover, and freeze for 2 hours.

3 Remove from the freezer and whiz the mixture again until really smooth to remove any ice crystals that may have formed.

4 Return to the freezer for at least 2 hours, until firm. Alternatively, spoon into ice-cube trays, cover with foil or put into a freezer bag, seal, and freeze.

5 Serve immediately or leave to soften for 5–10 minutes before serving.

drop scones

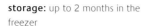

makes: 20 baby portions

storage: up to 2 months in the freezer

225g self-raising flour
1 large, free-range egg
300ml formula milk or
    calcium-enriched soya drink
15g unsalted butter, melted

To make these scones more exciting, try adding a pinch of ground cinnamon and a few tablespoons of blueberries or finely chopped banana. These are just as good for breakfast as they are for a pudding. Once you have defrosted the drop scones, they are best warmed briefly in an oven at 150°C/300°F/gas mark 2 before serving. This is only suitable for babies who are confident with chewing.

1 Sift the flour into a bowl. Whisk together the egg and half the milk. Make a well in the centre of the flour and pour in the egg mixture. Using a whisk, gradually beat the mixture until all the flour is incorporated and you have a thick batter. Gradually beat in the remaining milk.

2 Lightly brush a heavy-based frying pan with melted butter and heat. Drop small teaspoons of the mixture into the pan. Cook over a medium heat until the top of each scone bubbles (approximately 2-3 minutes), then flip it over using a palette knife. Cook for a further 2 minutes.

3 Repeat until all the mixture is used up. Eat immediately or freeze, putting greaseproof paper between the layers of scones.

4 To serve, thaw thoroughly and cut into tiny pieces.

apricot and hazelnut muesli bars

makes: 12 baby portions

storage: for up to 2 months in the freezer

Vitamin A

150g unsalted butter
50g golden caster sugar
125g golden syrup
250g porridge oats
25g hazelnuts
50g dried apricots (only for
    9-month-old babies plus)

These are definitely for older babies, especially those who are teething – they will love the chewy nuttiness of these bars. Because they are quite sweet, just give small pieces, ideally with a little fresh fruit on the plate, too. Remember, do not feed nuts to babies if there is a family history of allergies. This recipe is only suitable for babies who are confident with chewing.

1 Preheat the oven to 180°C/350°F/gas mark 4.

2 Put the butter, sugar, and syrup in a pan and heat until the butter has melted.

3 Put the oats, hazelnuts, and apricots into a food processor and whiz until ground.

4 Pour the oat mixture into the saucepan with the melted butter and mix well.

5 Tip into a greased baking tin (approx 35cm x 25cm), smooth the top, and bake until golden (approximately 10–15 minutes). Mark into squares with a knife and cool in the tin. Tip out of the tin, cut, and freeze or store in an airtight container for up to a week.

6 To serve, thaw thoroughly and break into very small pieces.

choc bread and butter pudding

 6½

 1

 1

1½

½

Vitamin B₁₂, A

1+

makes: 5–6 baby portions

storage: up to 2 months in the freezer

300g fruit bread, eg raisin bread, sliced and crusts removed (only for 9-month-old babies plus)

25g unsalted butter

3 tsp cocoa

25g golden caster sugar

1 tbsp boiling water

2 large, free-range eggs

568ml formula milk or calcium-enriched soya drink

This is a new version of a classic nursery pudding that children of all ages love. Remember, the chocolatey-ness of the finished dish will depend on the quality of cocoa you use; some cocoas are much stronger than others, so vary the amount accordingly.

1 Spread the fruit bread with the butter and cut into quarters in small triangles.
2 Lay half the triangles on the base of a buttered ovenproof dish.
3 In a mixing bowl, mix together the cocoa, sugar, and boiling water. Beat the eggs and milk together and add them to the cocoa mixture, mixing them together thoroughly.
4 Pour half of the milk mixture over the bread in the ovenproof dish. Arrange the remaining triangles over the top and pour the remaining liquid over them.
5 Leave to stand for 30 minutes to allow the bread to absorb the liquid. Wrap in foil and freeze.
6 To serve, thaw thoroughly. Preheat the oven to 170°C/325°F/gas mark 3. Bake in the oven for 35–40 minutes, until the top is crisp and golden. Mash for babies who are not confident with chewing.

banana and cinnamon teabread

2½

½

½

Vitamin B₁₂, A

1+

makes: 8–10 baby portions

storage: up to 2 months in the freezer

150g unsalted butter

100g golden caster sugar

2 medium, free-range eggs

2 ripe small bananas, mashed

2 tbsp formula milk or calcium-enriched soya drink

4 tbsp natural Greek yogurt

pinch ground cinnamon

150g self-raising flour

½ tsp baking powder

This is a great bread because it's not too sweet – the bananas are a natural sweetener. Try to use really ripe, black-spotted fruits because they will give the best flavour. My children love a slice of this spread with a mashed banana and cut into fingers. This is only suitable for babies who are confident with chewing.

1 Preheat the oven to 180°C/350°F/gas mark 4.
2 Cream the butter and sugar together until pale and fluffy. Beat in the eggs. Add the mashed bananas, milk, yogurt, and cinnamon and mix well.
3 Sift the flour and baking powder over the mixture and fold in.
4 Pour the mixture into a lightly greased 500g loaf tin and bake for 55–65 minutes, until a skewer inserted in the centre comes out clean. Slice and freeze with greaseproof paper between the slices. Alternatively, store in an airtight container for a few days.
5 To serve, thaw thoroughly and cut into tiny pieces.

As your baby approaches toddlerhood, mealtimes will become more exciting and involving for him. He should have an established routine, with healthy snacks and finger foods in between meals to maintain the energy levels needed for this period of rapid growth and development. As his co-ordination increases, he will develop skills such as being able to feed himself – albeit messily – that will enable him to participate more fully in family meals. This will give him a sense of his place in the world, a feeling of security and confidence in his abilities.

10-12 months

what's happening
to your baby

This is the stage at which your baby really begins to appreciate the routine of mealtimes, making him feel more secure and like part of the family – especially if you eat as many meals together as possible. His coordination and appreciation of colour and texture will also be developing. He will be able to point at objects, pick things up with his finger and thumb, and maybe even put things into and out of his bowl.

At mealtimes your baby can start to learn to feed himself, and will particularly enjoy feeding himself finger foods. He will be able to hold a feeder cup to drink from. He will also learn to let go of things deliberately, things may start to get messy, but this is when your baby really begins to learn about and appreciate good food. Get into the habit of feeding him foods that you enjoy – my daughter Jasmin's love of spicy food began at about 10 months, when I gave her a little of my favourite Thai green curry.

Your child will now have a sense of humour; even saying "boo" will make him laugh. He will enjoy playing, especially at bath time, and hearing you sing nursery rhymes will be a great source of entertainment to him. He may be able to say "mama" and "dada", and can indicate what he wants by gesturing instead of crying, both of which will make play more exciting.

Your baby is likely to begin to explore the world on foot by around 11 months, and it is important not to rush this. Often he will move by holding on to pieces of furniture and negotiating small distances between them with a little help from you. He may even be able to stand alone for a few seconds and will gradually learn to walk unaided.

However, it is also at this stage that babies begin to assert their independence by saying "no"! Your baby will also begin to understand the word "no" when you say it, but won't necessarily obey it. Try not to get too frustrated. At mealtimes, having smaller amounts of food on the plate often helps; otherwise, just take the food away and don't be tempted to offer sweet alternatives. Try creating interest at mealtimes by involving your baby in the preparation – even if it is only watching you chop carrots. For snacks, give food that can easily be held by small fingers – steamed carrot sticks are great.

At this stage it is important to encourage your baby to eat new things to ensure he is getting a wide range of nutrients. Adequate energy will be crucial for him as he starts to crawl and move about. Fat will be an essential energy-dense nutrient in the diet. Remember, it's the quality of the fat that matters – try using more unsaturated fats.

As your baby is crawling, he'll need more energy-rich food, particularly at the start of the day. Foods such as cereals and fresh fruits that are rich in slow-releasing carbohydrates are best for breakfast because they give your baby a steady flow of energy until his next feed. Many mums see all types of sugar as an easy way to give their baby energy; sugar is a carbohydrate, but it gives only short bursts of energy and has little nutritional value, so ideally it should be avoided. Sugar is also a major cause of tooth decay, to which first teeth are susceptible. Too much sugar can lead to health problems such as obesity later in life. It is not necessary to add sugar to your baby's food, even when foods are tart; just use other ripe fruits or apple juice to sweeten them.

Protein is essential for the healthy growth of every single one of the body's cells, and it is constantly being used and replaced. Because your baby is growing so rapidly, he will need more protein in relation to his weight than an adult. Good sources of protein for babies at this stage include meat, poultry, fish, full-fat dairy products, eggs, beans, pulses, soya products such as tofu, and calcium-enriched soya drinks and yogurt alternatives. Protein from animal sources is generally a complete protein; vegetarian and vegan babies need a combination of cereals, pulses and vegetables to get complete protein, as no non-animal source but tofu is a complete protein.

To help keep your baby's bowel movements regular, begin to introduce a little fibre in his diet. His digestive system is still immature and he will not be able to cope with the bulky fibre found in brown rice, wholewheat and bran. Instead, include foods such as peas, fruits and vegetable juices, which are easier for his system to tolerate. Also ensure he drinks enough liquid, as too little fluid is one of the main causes of constipation in babies.

which nutrients **are key**

nutrients required per day

At this stage, different formula milks provide different proportions of each nutrient required. For this book, we've assumed the lowest level provided by the common brands on which the milk chart on page 21 is based. The quantity of formula given is based on the recommended quantity (page 139). Assume breastfed babies receive the equivalent nutrient intake from milk. Solids play a greater role in the provision of nutrients now.
* If your baby enjoys a healthy balanced diet, he'll probably get more protein and vitamin C than he needs. Do not worry.

	Protein 1 point = 1.5 grams	Iron 1 point = 1.5mg	Zinc 1 point = 1mg	Calcium 1 point = 105mg	Vitamin C 1 point = 5mg
total points recommended	10 (14.9g)	5 (7.8mg)	5 (5mg)	5 (525mg)	5 (25mg)
milk (500ml of formula) provides	4½ (7g)	1½ (2.5mg)	2½ (2.5mg)	2 (230mg)	8 (41mg)
points required from food	5½ (*see caption)	3½	2½	3	0 (*see caption)

third-stage
weaning

Your baby should be still having 500–600ml of breast milk or formula milk a day, but his solid food will be just as important as a source of nutrition. Breakfast should be his biggest meal, giving him lots of energy. This should be an easy habit to get into because he will be at his hungriest after a good night's sleep. Make use of baby-friendly, sugar-free cereals and whiz them in a food processor to make their texture easier for your baby to cope with. Finely ground nuts (as long as there is no history of allergy in your family), are a valuable source of protein, especially for vegetarians.

Between meals, your baby should be given cooled, boiled water to drink from a cup and healthy snacks to maintain his energy levels. Finger foods have a harder texture now, especially as your baby begins to teethe. Give bread and even toast or home-made rusks once your baby is confident with chewing. Steamed vegetables sticks – and even raw sticks of softer vegetables such as cucumber – can be given, but always stay nearby in case your baby chokes. At this stage you baby will be able to cope with dried fruit, although it can cause upset stomachs so I still wouldn't get too carried away. If you want to reduce the amount of aritifical preservatives in your baby's diet, try and buy organic dried fruit or, at the very least, fruit that has not been treated with preservatives. Sulphur dioxide, the most commonly used preservative, has been shown to contribute to the causes of asthma in young children.

It is important to reduce your baby's milk intake to allow more room in his small tummy for solid food. Often parents are tempted to give milk when a baby of this age cries; try to give him solid foods instead – they will keep him satisfied for longer. One of the best ways to reduce milk intake is to dilute the mid-morning feed with cooled, boiled water; do this gradually as you reduce his overall milk consumption. Giving milk and other drinks in cups rather than bottles will help, and is recommended for the development of a baby's healthy teeth.

As your baby's appreciation of colour and texture develops, give him foods that will stimulate his senses and not just his appetite. Brightly coloured finger foods, such as steamed carrot sticks, were always a hit with my children. Try adding peas or little pieces of carrot to mash, or serving chopped fruit with a different coloured fruit purée. But remember, babies develop at different paces, and some can chew earlier than others, so use your own judgement and never leave your baby alone with food at any time.

Food can now be minced or finely chopped. You can give your baby almost all the foods you eat yourself; just remember not to season them with salt during cooking and to finely chop them. It is a good idea to introduce new foods in small quantities and with something familiar so that your baby does not feel overwhelmed. The main aim of this stage of weaning is to be able to include your baby at all the family meals and not have to cook separate meals for him, although obviously you will have to chop or mash as necessary. Many of the recipes in this book are suitable for the whole family.

Most importantly, you can begin to introduce foods that have more intense flavours. Herbs, such as parsley, oregano, basil, and coriander, give standard dishes a much more interesting flavour. Onions and garlic can be used, as well as mild spices such as cinnamon and ginger, and the ever-popular vanilla pod. These natural ingredients will encourage your child to enjoy a variety of tastes and show him that delicious flavours can be natural rather than artificial.

Bottles for drinks other than milk should be phased out at this stage, primarily to ensure healthy teeth. Drinks from cups will be drunk quicker than those from a bottle, minimizing the time they are in contact with a baby's vulnerable first teeth. This is especially important if you are giving diluted fruit juices, which should never be given in a bottle. It is also good to begin to teach your baby how to hold a cup and drink with other children and adults; it will make him feel part of the family. Always make sure you wash the spout of a drinking cup regularly (see pages 28–29).

common myths

myth: snacks are bad
Babies and children have small stomachs and expend a lot of energy. Snacking is an easy way for them to top up their energy levels without spoiling their appetite for bigger meals. Many of the huge range of snacks available for babies and children are sugary and highly processed with additives to make them palatable. This is the perfect time, while your baby is not influenced by peer pressure, to encourage him to nibble on healthy snacks, such as steamed or lightly cooked vegetable sticks, fingers of bread and fresh fruits.

myth: fat is bad
While saturated fat is not so healthy, every baby's diet should include unsaturated fat. They need the calories for energy and to absorb fat-soluble vitamins.

myth: it's healthy to give fresh fruit juice between meals
Freshly squeezed fruit juices contain more nutrients than fruit-flavoured squashes or fizzy drinks, but first teeth are particularly susceptible to damage from the sugar all these drinks contain. A small amount of freshly squeezed juice, preferably non-citrus, is fine, but always dilute it and give it at mealtimes in a cup rather than a bottle to minimize the time the drink is in contact with teeth. Cooled, boiled water is best for quenching thirst.

foods to eat and
foods to avoid

new foods to eat at 10-12 months

It's important to remember that babies develop at different paces, and they should never be left alone with food at any time.

- As the amount of solid food in your baby's diet increases, he will need some fibre to help keep his bowel movements regular. Soluble fibre, found in foods such as peas, fruit and vegetable juices, is sufficient because his immature digestive system will not be able to cope with the bulky fibre found in brown rice and whole wheat.
- At least one baby portion of animal protein or its vegetable equivalent should be given each day. A wider range of fish can be introduced, especially oily fish such as mackerel and tuna (but not in brine).
- Whole well-cooked eggs.
- Small amounts of full-fat cow's milk, but only as part of a larger dish, such as custard.

foods to avoid at 10-12 months

- Cow's milk or soya milk as a drink.
- If there is any history of allergy in your family, avoid nuts, nut products or foods containing nuts until your child is at least 3 years old and seek professional advice from your doctor or state-registered dietitian. Whole peanuts should never be given to children under the age of 5 as there is a risk of choking.
- Shellfish can trigger allergic reactions in young babies, especially if there's a history of it in their family.
- Unpasteurized cheese may contain the bacteria listeria that can cause food poisoning. Babies are more sensitive to this bacteria.
- Too much salt can't be processed by a baby's immature digestive system; it causes dehydration. A diet high in salt often leads to high blood pressure later. Particular foods to avoid at this stage are yeast extracts, such as marmite or vegemite, stock cubes, and smoked fish (see page 90).
- Refined or unrefined sugar provides calories but has little nutritional value. Always give sweet things, such as fruit, at mealtimes so the acid that damages teeth is diluted; cheese is particularly good at doing this. Check food labels carefully since sugar may be present as sucrose, glucose, fructose, lactose, hydrolyzed starch, invert sugar, and products such as treacle, honey, and syrup.
- Never use artificial sweeteners.
- Avoid honey until your baby is 1; it may contain botulism spores that can cause food poisoning.
- Excessively hot or spicy foods can burn or inflame babies' stomachs.
- Tea and coffee contain tannins inhibit iron absorption. Caffeine is a stimulant, which babies cannot tolerate. Most fizzy drinks also contain caffeine.

A 10-month-old baby will begin to appreciate the routine of meal times, making him feel more secure and part of the family – especially if you eat as many meals together as possible.

Three key changes to a baby's diet take place at 10 months. The first is his milk intake; it is important to reduce this in order to allow more room in his small tummy for solid food. Often parents are tempted to give milk when a baby of this age cries; try to give solids instead – they will keep him satisfied for longer as he becomes more active. But be sure to give your baby plenty of liquids aside from milk, such as water and juice, to avoid constipation.

The second key change is the balance of nutrition. Immune-boosting foods continue to be important, but the real focus is on strength. Your baby needs more starch, protein, sugar and fats to enable him to build up the strength to crawl and walk.

The third key change is volume. Your baby is likely to start really enjoying food now. His coordination and appreciation of colour and texture will be developing, so try to encourage him to eat well by giving him lots of variety. However, it is also at this stage that babies begin to assert their independence by saying "no". Try not to get too frustrated over this; having smaller amounts of food on the plate often helps prevent it; otherwise, just take the food away and don't be tempted to offer your baby sweet alternatives.

recommended **daily intake**

recommended daily volume of foods

milk = breastfeed or 150ml formula

	10 months old	11 months old	12 months old
breakfast	breastfeed or milk from a cup, alternating during feed with 1 portion breakfast and 1 portion fruit, water	breastfeed or milk from a cup, alternating during feed with 1-2 portions breakfast	breastfeed or milk from a cup, alternating during feed with 1-2 portions breakfast
lunch	1 portion lunch, also sometimes 1 portion pudding or snack, water or well-diluted fruit juice from a cup	1 portion lunch, also sometimes 1 portion pudding or snack, water or well-diluted fruit juice from a cup	1 portion lunch, also sometimes 1 portion pudding or snack, water or well-diluted fruit juice from a cup
mid-pm	milk or water, alternating during feed with 1 portion snack or finger food	milk or water, 1 portion snack or finger food	milk or water, 1 portion snack or finger food
supper	1 portion supper, also sometimes 1 portion pudding, water, milk	1 portion supper, also sometimes 1 portion pudding, water, milk	1 portion supper, 1 portion pudding, water
10pm	small milk feed if needed	small milk feed if needed	small milk feed if needed
TOTAL MILK	breast milk or 500-600ml formula each day, inclusive of milk used in sauces, cereals, etc	breast milk or 500-600ml formula each day, inclusive of milk used in sauces, cereals, etc	breast milk or 400-500ml formula each day, inclusive of milk used in sauces, cereals, etc

your
routine

your baby's feeds

Solid food is becoming nutritionally more important each day, week, and month of your baby's life. By 10 months, your baby should be quite comfortable with eating a wide range of solid foods, and he should be enjoying three meals, ideally with the rest of the family, by the time he is 1 year old.

You may begin to notice that your baby does not want to drink all of his bedtime milk feed. If this does start to happen, you will need to stop the mid-afternoon milk feed if you have not already done so. If he is already having water in the afternoon, then make sure that he is not eating too many solid foods or snacks at this time instead. This is important because he still needs to be drinking his evening milk feed to make sure that he sleeps through the night.

your baby's sleeps

If your baby is still having a quick nap (anything up to 45 minutes) in the morning after breakfast, you may start to notice that he is waking up earlier after his lunchtime sleep. Rather than having two short naps, I would try to stop the early morning sleep and keep to one long sleep, approximately 1½–2¼ hours, after lunch. Ideally, try to make sure he is up and awake from 2.30pm to be confident that he will go to sleep successfully from bedtime at around 7pm. Aim to get him into a routine of just one sleep by the time he is 1 year old at the latest.

coping with fussy eaters

As your baby learns to assert his independence he may begin to say "no" to certain foods, often pushing them away. While this will be frustrating for you, try not to show disappointment. Try again briefly and, if his mouth remains closed, just remove the food and don't offer an alternative, especially not anything sweet, because this will only create problems.

throwing food on the floor

As your baby becomes more coordinated he can begin to learn to feed himself. He may throw food onto the floor, which is often a sign that he has had enough or is bored with the food. Try adding interest by introducing new textures and flavours. If throwing persists, just take the food away and never offer alternatives – children eat sweet foods even if they are full.

spills from self-feeding

As your baby learns to feed himself, there may be a lot of spills. Try giving him a spoon to hold with a little food on it, or a stick of finger food, while you feed him with a separate spoon – he will get enough to eat but feel he has some control over proceedings. The more you let him try to feed himself, the quicker he will become more coordinated.

worries about food at the childminders

If you are sending your baby to a childminder or nursery and you are concerned about the food that he is being fed, just send your baby with food for the day. Every childminder and nursery is different and each will feed babies and toddlers what they feel is the right sort of food. However, nearly all of them will be more than willing to feed your baby with food you have provided, should you wish to do so. This way you can be certain that she will be getting exactly the right sort of diet.

refusal to eat at mealtimes

If your baby is not willing to eat at mealtimes or messes with his food and does not concentrate on eating, there may be a simple answer. Some babies just prefer to have company when eating and enjoy watching and mimicking others. Even if it is the wrong time of day for you to eat a meal, it may be worth eating a little so that he does not feel he is eating alone.

trouble
shooting

sample meal planners

key to meal planners

each milk feed:
Breastfeed or 200ml formula
portions:
After 5 months, all servings of food referred to in the meal planners is 1 portion
water:
Always give cooled, boiled water or very dilute fruit juice. After 9 months, all drinks should be served in a beaker.
mealtimes
breakfast 7-8am
lunch 11.45-ish
mid-afternoon 3pm
supper 6.30pm-ish, for bed at 7pm-ish

At 10-12 months, solids are as important a source of nutrition as milk. On page 135 you'll find a chart showing how much of each of the key nutrients your child generally needs to obtain from solid food. For some of these nutrients, in particular protein, you'll inevitably significantly exceed these recommended intakes if you cook your baby fresh food – do not worry, as this will not harm your child. Equally, do not worry if your baby doesn't get enough points every single day, as all babies have cranky days. The important thing is to ensure that, on average your baby is getting the recommended intake. If your baby is getting a good variety and mix of foods, all other essential nutrients which we haven't allocated points to should be more than covered.

The key things you need to achieve during these months are making breakfast the biggest meal of the day and giving your baby healthy snacks between meals – you'll find lots of quick ideas on pages 178-181. And, of course, you still need to provide plenty of cooled, boiled water between meals. You can now aim to include your baby in all the family mealtimes, as he can enjoy most of the foods that the whole family eats – just remember to remove his portion before adding salt.

10 months old, any week

	breakfast	lunch	mid-afternoon	supper	10pm
day 1	plum and ginger yogurt, water, then milk	cheese and ham on toast, water	milk, alternated with cucumber sticks, water	lamb chops with pea mash, water, milk	small milk if needed
day 2	really quick muesli, water, then milk	stuffed baked potatoes, water	milk, alternated with apricots and cream cheese, water	fish baked in orange juice, water, milk	small milk if needed
day 3	French toast with cinnamon, water, then milk	leek and ham mash, water	milk, alternated with apple and raisin toast, water	leek/chive macaroni, nutty yogurt, water, milk	small milk if needed
day 4	fresh and dried fruit compote, water, then milk	peanut noodles, rice pud with dried fruits, water	milk, alternated with dried fruit/vanilla yogurt, water	sweet potato gratin, mango/raspberry soup, water, milk	small milk if needed
day 5	fruity couscous, water, then milk	tuna and tomato mash, water	milk, alternated with steamed veg sticks, water	chicken goujons, berry sponge, water, milk	small milk if needed
day 6	tropical yogurt, water, then milk	broccoli, chicken, rice, muesli bar yogurt, water	milk, alternated with rice cakes, water	tortolloni, strawberries and passion fruit, water, milk	small milk if needed
day 7	chunky spiced apple sauce, water, then milk	lamb burgers, water	milk, alternated with pieces of banana, water	Moroccan beef, water, milk	small milk if needed

11 months old, any day

	breakfast	lunch	mid-afternoon	supper	10pm
day 1	blueberry and cinnamon porridge, water, then milk	chickpea and bacon stew, water	milk, alternated with apple flapjack, water	sardines on toast, baked almond peach, water, milk	small milk if needed
day 2	fig and honey yogurt, toast, water, then milk	curried parsnip soup, muesli bar with yogurt, water	milk, alternated with pieces of apple, water	ham and pea pasta, apple flapjack, water, milk	small milk if needed
day 3	scrambled eggs, toasted bun, water, then milk	pesto and pea mash, water	milk, alternated steamed veg/cottage cheese, water	beans, tuna and cheese; muesli bar; water, milk	small milk if needed
day 4	papaya and coconut lassi; easy muesli, water, milk	Spanish tortilla; fruit smush, water	milk, alternated with pitta bread fingers, water	cottage pie, water, milk	small milk if needed
day 5	chunky plum yogurt, toast, water, then milk	tuna pasta, water	milk, alternated with malt loaf with mashed bananas, water	savoury crumble, vanilla pears, water, milk	small milk if needed
day 6	toast with bacon and tomatoes, water, then milk	beetroot and spinach with rice, apple flapjack, water	milk alternated with popcorn, water	baked bean gratin, fruit with cream cheese, water, milk	small milk if needed
day 7	banana porridge, water, then milk	pasta with cheese and bacon, water	milk, alternated with pieces of pear, water	home-made fish fingers, rice pudding, water, milk	small milk if needed

12 months old, any day

	breakfast	lunch	mid-afternoon	supper	10pm
day 1	carrot/pineapple smoothie, vanilla porridge, water, milk	fish and courgette gratin, nutty yogurt, water	milk, alternated with raisins	eastern rice with veg, baked bananas, water, milk	small milk if needed
day 2	fruit muffin, water, then milk	sweetcorn/ham mash. rice pud with dried fruits, water	milk, alternated with popcorn	pasta, spinach/cheese, apple/ Cheddar crackers, water, milk	small milk if needed
day 3	coconut muesli with banana, water, then milk	pasta with pesto and peas, water	milk, alternated with raw vegetable sticks	baked beans with sausage, water, milk	small milk if needed
day 4	potato scramble, water, then milk	tomato risotto, water	milk, alternated with dried apricots	green bean with tuna gratin, tropical fruits with raspberry sauce, water, milk	small milk if needed
day 5	creamy banana toast, water, then milk	bacon and mushrooms in cheese, water	milk, alternated with baby tomato pieces	chicken/sesame balls, banana/ apple crumble, water, milk	small milk if needed
day 6	nut bread, water, then milk	chickpeas and bacon stew, water	milk, alternated with cream cheese soldiers	mushroom and bacon ragu, fruit trifle, water, milk	small milk if needed
day 7	scrambled eggs with bacon, water, then milk	cheese and corn muffins, water	milk, alternated with satsuma segments	sausage, apple, parsnip pie, autumn rice pud, water, milk	small milk if needed

fresh breakfasts

coconut muesli with banana

 3

 1

 1½

 ½

 1

Vitamin B₁

makes: 20 baby portions or a mixture of baby and adult portions

storage: keep in an airtight container for up to 4 weeks

75g hazelnuts or almonds
50g sunflower seeds
50g desiccated coconut
4 tbsp wheatgerm
300g rolled porridge oats
pinch of ground cinnamon
100g dried fruit, eg dried
** cranberries, raisins or**
** apricots, finely chopped**
breast milk, formula milk or
** full-fat cow's milk, to serve**
½ medium banana or mango,
** finely chopped or mashed,**
** to serve (optional)**

As your baby grows, he will start to enjoy slightly more challenging textures. Muesli is a great way to incorporate a wide variety of nuts, seeds, and oats into his diet: all fantastic sources of protein and energy-providers. Make a large batch of this muesli and keep it in an airtight tin; just make sure you buy the ingredients from a shop with a good turnover so they are as fresh as possible. Do not give nuts or seeds to babies if there is any family history of allergies.

1. Dry-fry the nuts and seeds in a frying pan, stirring constantly until golden brown (approximately 5 minutes). Cool.
2. Transfer to a food processor, add the coconut and wheatgerm, and whiz to a powder. Tip into a bowl, add the oats and cinnamon, and mix everything together.
3. Finely chop the dried fruit, then put a pan on the hob with 4-5 tbsp water and cook for approximately 5 minutes. Beat the fruit to a purée.
4. Spoon 5-6 tbsp of the muesli into a bowl, pour over some milk and top with the dried fruit purée and mashed banana, if using.
5. Leave to sit for 5 minutes to soften slightly before serving

plum and ginger yogurt

 2

½

½

 1+

Vitamin B₁

makes: 3 baby portions or 1 baby portion and 1 adult portions

storage: up to 48 hours in the refrigerator

1cm fresh root ginger
5 ripe red plums, stoned
2 tbsp natural full-fat yogurt

Note: do not feed chopped food to your baby until he is confident with chewing.

Fresh ginger has a hot flavour and is known for its stimulating and warming properties. It is particularly helpful for fighting off colds and chills. If you can't find any, just use a little pinch of dried ginger instead.

1. Peel the ginger, then put into a saucepan with the plums and 2–3 tbsp water. Cook gently for 5–10 minutes, or until plums are soft.
2. Remove the ginger. Leave the plums to cool and then mash if necessary. Mix 2 tbsp with the same amount of yogurt.

toast with bacon and tomatoes

6

1

1½

2

Vitamin B₁

makes: 1 baby portion

storage: best eaten immediately

1 rasher unsmoked back bacon, preferably organic, rind removed
1 ripe tomato, halved
1 slice brown bread

When you are cooking for babies, it is important to use good-quality meat. They eat such small amounts that it is especially worthwhile. Good bacon should cook without a white scum forming on the surface – this scum is made up of added salt, water, and preservatives.

1 Preheat the grill on high.

2 Grill the bacon and tomato until the bacon is cooked through but not too crispy, and the tomato is soft.

3 Toast the bread. Place the tomato halves cut-side down on the toast, peel away their skin, and mash the flesh onto the toast. Cut the toast into soldiers.

4 Cut the bacon into small pieces and scatter over the top.

really quick muesli

5

1

1½

2

Vitamin B₁

makes: 15 baby portions or a mixture of baby and adult portions

storage: keep in an airtight container for up to 4 weeks

2 tbsp sesame seeds, ground
2 tbsp poppy seeds, ground
50g ground almonds
200g rolled or porridge oats
pinch of ground nutmeg
100g dried fruits, eg mango or pear, finely chopped
natural full-fat yogurt, to serve (optional)

This is so easy – and a delicious alternative to all those high-in-sugar, packaged cereals for all the family. Home-made muesli can be stored for up to four weeks in a jar or airtight tin. Remember, do not give nuts or seeds to babies if there is any family history of allergies.

1 Dry-fry the ground sesame seeds, poppy seeds, and almonds for a couple of minutes. Transfer to a bowl and cool.

2 Add the oats and nutmeg.

3 Cook the dried fruits in 5 tbsp water for approximately 5 minutes, then purée.

4 Sprinkle 4-5 tbsp muesli over 4 tbsp yogurt, top with the purée, and serve.

french toast with cinnamon

4

½

½

Vitamin B₁₂

1⁺

makes: 2 baby portions or 1 baby portion and 1 small adult portion

storage: best eaten immediately

1 large free-range egg, lightly beaten

1 tbsp full-fat milk

drop of vanilla extract

knob of unsalted butter, for greasing

3-4 slices fruit bread

pinch of ground cinnamon

You can make this as a savoury breakfast instead of a sweet one simply by omitting the cinnamon and vanilla and using ordinary bread – or a loaf with herbs, onion or cheese.

1 Put the egg, milk, and vanilla in a bowl and whisk together.

2 Heat a frying pan over a medium heat and then grease it with a little unsalted butter.

3 Dip 2 slices of bread into the egg mixture and put into the hot frying pan. Cook the bread for 2 minutes on each side, until golden. Repeat with the remaining bread.

4 Cut into pieces and sprinkle with cinnamon.

scrambled egg with a toasted bun

7

1

1

1

Vitamin B₁₂, A

1⁺

makes: 1 baby portion

storage: best eaten immediately

small knob of unsalted butter

2 large free-range eggs

2–3 tbsp full-fat milk or calcium-enriched soya drink

freshly ground black pepper (optional)

1 tbsp fresh herbs (optional), chopped

1 fresh wholemeal bun

unsalted butter, for spreading

Scrambled eggs are one of the quickest and most versatile meals for all the family – this could just as easily be served for lunch or supper. For breakfast, keeping it simple is often best, but you can add lots of things to scrambled eggs: peas, chopped herbs (especially chives), mushrooms – the list is endless.

1 Melt the butter in a non-stick pan. Whisk the eggs and milk together and season with a little black pepper and fresh herbs, if using.

2 Pour the eggs into the pan and cook over a gentle heat, stirring constantly until they are scrambled and well cooked, with no runny bits.

3 Slice the bun in half and toast until just pale golden, then spread with a little butter.

4 Cut one half of the bun into small pieces. Top with half the scrambled egg. Serve the remaining bun and scrambled egg on a plate for you.

quick bites breakfasts

2 ½ ½ 1½ 2

tropical yogurt

½ small mango, peeled and roughly chopped
70g natural full-fat yogurt
1 tbsp unsweetened shredded coconut

Mash the mango with a fork and mix into the yogurt with the coconut. For older children, split open a fresh coconut and just peel and grate the flesh. Do not serve coconut to babies if there is any family history of allergies.

1 ½ 2

fig yogurt

1 fresh fig
50g natural full-fat yogurt

Cut the fig in half and scrape out the flesh, then mash with the yogurt. This is also good spread on toast.

½ ½ 2

chunky plum yogurt

1 slice raisin bread
70ml natural full-fat yogurt
1 plum, stoned and finely chopped

Lightly toast the bread and cut it into small pieces. Stir it into the yogurt with the chopped plum. If the mixture is a little thick, thin it with some breast milk, formula milk or full-fat milk. Leave to soak for at least 10 minutes. (The longer you leave this, the softer the toast will become.)

3 ½ 1 2½

hazelnut milk and banana smoothie

50g skinned hazelnuts
250ml cold water
½ ripe banana, peeled and chopped

Whiz the nuts and water with a hand-held blender for 2-3 minutes, until you get a thick milk. Add the fruit and whiz again. For smaller babies, pass through a nylon sieve. Do not serve nuts to babies if there is any family history of allergies.

1 ½ 1 ½ 3

creamy banana toast

50g full-fat cream cheese
½ banana
1 piece wholemeal toast

Mash the cream cheese with the banana and spread on the toast. Try cream cheese and peanut butter, too, so long as there is no family history of allergies.

8 1 1 1 4

weetabix with strawberries and yogurt

1 Weetabix
70–90ml full-fat milk
1 tbsp natural Greek yogurt
50g strawberries, mashed

Weetabix are great because they go mushy naturally in milk. Adding fresh fruit will considerably increase the vitamin content of your baby's breakfast. Crumble the Weetabix into a bowl. Add the milk, yogurt, and strawberries and mix everything together.

blueberry and cinnamon porridge

2 C ½ 🥛 ½ 🐟 ½ 🐟 2 🥚

50g prepared porridge (see page 96)
30g blueberries, mashed
pinch of ground cinnamon

When you are making porridge for the rest of the family, just weigh out some for your baby. Mix it with the blueberries and cinnamon.

banana porridge

1 C ½ 🥛 ½ 🐟 2 🥚

50g prepared porridge (see page 96)
½ ripe medium banana, finely chopped, or roughly mashed

Porridge is really versatile – you can add almost any fruit to it. Sometimes adding banana can make it quite thick, so you may need to thin with a little full-fat milk.

fruity couscous

1 C ½ 🐟 1 🥚

100ml fresh orange juice
30g couscous
50g raspberries, mashed

Heat the orange juice in a pan to just below boiling point and then pour it over the couscous. Leave to soak for 5 minutes, fluff with a fork, then add the mashed raspberries.

papaya and coconut milk lassi

✓ 2½ C 1 🥛 ½ 🐟 2 🥚

Vitamin B₁₂

½ ripe papaya, peeled and chopped
50ml coconut milk
50ml natural full-fat yogurt
50ml full-fat milk

Put all the ingredients together in a bowl and whiz with a hand-held blender (or in a food processor or blender) until smooth. Lassis are great because they are less acidic than smoothies. You can use pretty much any soft fruit to make this drink. Do not serve coconut to babies if there is any family history of allergies.

carrot and pineapple smoothie

✓ 2½ C 1½ 🥛 ½ 🥚

Vitamin A

100g fresh pineapple, peeled
100ml carrot juice, fresh if possible
½ banana, chopped
1 tsp fresh ginger, peeled and grated

Cut the pineapple into chunks. Put all the ingredients into a bowl and whiz with a hand-held blender (or in a food processor or blender) until smooth. Add the fresh ginger for a zingy smoothie that will help to keep colds at bay.

potato scramble

1½ C ½ 🥛 2 🐟 1 🐟 6 🥚

75g potato, peeled, boiled
tiny knob of unsalted butter
1 large free-range egg, beaten
chopped fresh parsley (optional)

Chop the potatoes into small pieces. Melt the butter in a heavy-based frying pan and fry the potato until it is just golden. Add the egg and cook, stirring often with a wooden spoon until the egg is well cooked, with no runny bits. Add a little chopped fresh parsley if you have some to hand.

scrambled eggs with bacon

✓ 1 🐟 1½ 🐟 6½ 🥚

Vitamin B₁, B₁₂, A

1 rasher unsmoked back bacon, grilled
3–4 tbsp scrambled egg, made with a little full-fat milk and unsalted butter (see page 147)

Cut the rind off the bacon, then finely chop the bacon and stir into the scrambled eggs. You could also add chopped herbs, cooked mushrooms, grated cheese or grilled tomato. Ensure the eggs are well cooked, with no runny bits.

All quick bites make 1 portion unless otherwise stated.

breakfasts to freeze

bacon and apple bread

3

½

½

1

Vitamin B₁₂

1+

makes: 10 baby portions
(1kg loaf)

storage: up to 3 months in the
freezer

2 rashers unsmoked back
bacon

200g self-raising flour

½ tsp baking powder

1 eating apple, peeled and
grated

2 tbsp fresh parsley, chopped

4 tbsp olive oil

1 medium free-range egg

85ml full-fat milk

50g medium Cheddar
cheese, grated

This is a lovely, moist scone bread that freezes fantastically. It is great on its own or spread with cream cheese or mashed banana. Choose unsmoked bacon, which will have a less overpowering flavour – I have added only a small amount of bacon because it is quite high in salt.

1   Preheat the oven to 180°C/350°F/gas mark 4. Grease and lightly flour a 1kg loaf tin.
2   Grill the bacon until crisp, then cut into very small pieces.
3   Sieve the flour and baking powder into a bowl. Stir in the apple, parsley, and bacon, then make a well in the middle.
4   Mix together the oil, egg, milk, and cheese and pour into the well. Mix everything together but do not beat.
5   Spoon the mixture into the prepared tin and bake for 25 minutes until risen and golden.
6   Cool slightly and serve, or cool, slice, wrap each slice individually in foil, and freeze. To serve, thaw thoroughly.

banana scones

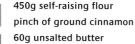

3

½

½

1+

makes: 20 baby portions

storage: up to 3 months in the
freezer

450g self-raising flour

pinch of ground cinnamon

60g unsalted butter

1 very ripe medium banana,
roughly mashed

284ml buttermilk

4–6 tbsp full-fat milk

Note: babies develop at
different rates; do not feed
chopped food to your baby until
he is confident with chewing.

Once you have made a batch of these, they are a great stand-by for mornings when time is really short. Scones are particularly good for teething babies – and a healthier alternative to shop-bought rusks. Try serving them with some chunks of banana or spread with a little mashed banana.

1   Preheat the oven to 180°C/350°F/gas mark 4.
2   Sieve the flour and cinnamon into a large bowl, then rub in the butter until the mixture resembles breadcrumbs. Stir in the banana and buttermilk.
3   Add enough milk to make a soft sticky dough. Drop little spoonfuls onto a greased baking sheet. Bake for 14-16 minutes, until golden and cooked.
4   Leave to cool on a wire rack.
5   Freeze in a freezerproof container. To serve, thaw thoroughly and cut into small pieces.

chunky spiced apple sauce

makes: 4–5 baby portions

storage: up to 2 months in the freezer

4 eating apples, eg Cox's orange pippin
pinch of allspice
4 dried apricots, finely chopped
12 tbsp water

This is a brilliant stand-by and is great served with yogurt, muesli, or baby rice. Only add enough sugar to take away the tartness of the apples. Remember your baby will have less of a sweet tooth than you.

1 Peel and core the apples and put into a saucepan with the allspice, apricots and water. Cook over a gentle heat until the apples are soft and pulpy (approximately 15-20 minutes). Stir often to prevent them sticking.

2 Cool and freeze in freezer bags or in a freezerproof container. Thaw thoroughly before using.

fruit muffins

makes: 15 baby portions

storage: up to 3 months in the freezer

150g plain flour
½ tsp baking powder
pinch of ground cinnamon
1 large free-range egg
125ml full-fat milk
50g unsalted butter, melted
75g golden caster sugar
125g fresh blueberries

You can make these with any soft fruit – blueberries, raspberries, apples or bananas – and in any combination. Use what is plentiful and cheap! They are a brilliant breakfast stand-by for all the family, and are especially good for packed lunches or picnics.

1 Preheat the oven to 200°C/400°F/gas mark 6. Grease a muffin tin or line with paper cases.

2 Sift the flour, baking powder, and cinnamon into a large bowl. In another large bowl, mix together the egg, milk, melted butter, sugar and blueberries.

3 Pour the flour mixture over the wet ingredients and quickly fold in – don't over-mix. The mixture should look lumpy and uneven.

4 Spoon the mixture into the prepared tin and bake for 15 minutes until risen and golden. Serve or cool on a wire rack and freeze.

5 To serve, heat through from frozen in an pre-heated oven at 180°C/350°F/gas mark 4 for 5-6 minutes and cut into small pieces.

nut bread

makes 10 baby portions

storage: up to 3 months in freezer

Vitamin B₁

400g plain white flour
400g wholemeal flour
50g hazelnuts, ground
25g sesame seeds, ground
25g sunflower seeds or
  flaked almonds, ground
approx. 360ml warm water
1 tsp golden caster sugar
6g (2 level tsp) dried yeast

This is a really easy bread to make, and it has a lovely nutty flavour. Once you get into the habit of breadmaking, it needn't take up much time and the results are so much nicer than shop-bought loaves. The quantities are easily doubled. Do not serve nuts or seeds to babies if there is any family history of allergies.

1 Grease a 1kg loaf tin.
2 Put the flour into a large bowl and mix in the nuts and seeds.
3 Put 100ml warm water into a measuring jug, stir in the sugar, then the yeast and leave somewhere warm for 10-15 minutes until a froth has formed on the top.
4 Make a well in the centre of the flour and pour in the yeast. Stir with a wooden spoon, gradually adding the rest of the warm water. Use your hands to form a smooth dough that comes away from the edges of the bowl, adding a little more water if necessary.
5 Knead the dough briefly for approximately 5 minutes on a floured surface and then shape into an oblong and drop into the prepared tin.
6 Sprinkle the loaf with flour, cover with a warm damp cloth and leave to rise in a warm place for 30-40 minutes.
7 Preheat the oven to 200°C/400°F/gas mark 4 then bake the bread for 40 minutes. Remove from the tin and bake upside down on a baking tray for 10-15 minutes to crisp up the sides and the bottom. When the loaf is cooked, it will sound hollow on the bottom when tapped.
8 Cool completely on a wire rack. Wrap in foil and freeze or slice and wrap each slice in foil and freeze. To serve, thaw thoroughly.

fresh and dried fruit compote

makes: 5-6 baby portions

storage: up to 2 months in freezer

3 dried apricots, finely
  chopped
50g dried apple, finely
  chopped
3 ready-to-eat prunes, finely
  chopped
100ml apple juice
50ml water
3-4 fresh pears, peeled,
  cored and finely chopped

This is great served with a little natural full-fat yogurt, apple purée or muesli. In the winter you can serve it warm, and it's also great served with porridge

1 Put the dried fruits, apple juice, and water into a saucepan.
2 Bring to the boil and simmer gently for 5 minutes.
3 Transfer to a bowl and add the fresh pears. Leave for at least 20 minutes.
4 Once cool, spoon into a freezer-proof container or freezer bags and freeze. To serve, thaw thoroughly.

fresh lunches

tomato risotto

3
½
½
1
½ **C**

1+

makes: 6 baby portions or 2 baby portions and 2 adult portions

storage: rice should not be reheated, but can be served cold up to 24 hour after cooking

25g unsalted butter
3 shallots, chopped finely
175g arborio rice
300ml of tomato passata or chopped tinned tomatoes
475ml light no-salt vegetable stock (very weak)
2 tbsp fresh basil, torn
50g Parmesan, grated

Make this at the weekend when everyone is at home, because it makes enough to feed a family of four. Alternatively, halve the quantities. This risotto is particularly easy because constant stirring isn't required – you just bung it in the oven.

1 Preheat the oven at 180°C/350°F/gas mark 4.
2 Melt the butter in a heavy-based pan and fry the shallots slowly, without colouring, until softened (approximately 5-10 minutes). Turn the heat up slightly and add the rice to the pan and stir, thoroughly coating it with the buttery shallots.
3 Stir for 1-2 minutes, until you hear the rice make a hissing sound, which means it's time to add the liquid. Add the tomato passata and stir well. Let it bubble and then add the stock and 1 tbsp basil. Bring up to simmering point, stir once, and transfer to a warm ovenproof dish, without covering. Put in the middle of oven. After 20 minutes, remove from the oven and stir once.
4 Return to the oven for 15 minutes. When the rice is cooked but has a little bite, stir in the Parmesan and remaining basil. Leave for 2 minutes, cool, then serve.

cheese and ham on toast

7½
1½
1
1

Vitamin B₁, A

1+

makes: 1 baby portions

storage: best eaten immediately

little knob of unsalted butter
2 slices white bread
2 slices cooked ham
50g medium Cheddar cheese, grated

Note: babies develop at different rates; do not feed chopped food to your baby until he is confident with chewing.

When you make this, toast only one side of the bread; this keeps the toast slightly softer than normal to compensate for the lack of teeth! Use a cheese with a decent flavour that also melts well, eg Cheddar, Cheshire or Lancashire.

1 Lightly butter the bread.
2 Chop the ham finely and scatter over the slices of bread.
3 Sprinkle the cheese on top and then grill until the bread is golden around the edges and the cheese has melted.
4 Cut into very small pieces.

spanish tortilla

6½

1

1

½

1½ C

Vitamin B₁, B₁₂, A

1+

makes: 4 baby portions or 2 baby portions and 1 adult portion

storage: best eaten immediately or up to 24 hours in the refrigerator

450g floury potatoes, peeled and halved

2 tbsp olive oil

1 onion, thinly sliced

4 large free-range eggs, beaten

This delicious potato omelette is wonderful with a sprinkling of finely chopped cooked ham or crumbled cooked bacon, or some quickly sautéed mushrooms to help to make it a little more substantial.

1 Bring a pan of water to the boil.
2 Cook the potatoes in the pan of boiling water until they are soft on the outside but still firm in the middle (approximately 5-7 minutes). Drain and cut into thin slices.
3 Heat the olive oil in a frying pan and add the sliced onion. Cook slowly for 10 minutes until the onion is soft. Add the sliced potatoes and cook for a further 5 minutes.
4 Preheat the grill to high.
5 Pour the beaten eggs over the potato and onion mixture and cook over a medium heat until it has set on the bottom. Put the pan under the grill to finish cooking the top.
6 Cut a quarter of the omelette into small pieces.

sweet potato hummus

4½

1½

1

1

2 C

Vitamin B₁, A

1+

makes: 3 baby portions

storage: 48 hours in the refrigerator

2 medium-sweet potatoes, well scrubbed

400g tin chickpeas, drained and rinsed

1 tbsp tahini

1 garlic clove, chopped

juice of ½ lemon

1 tbsp olive oil

to serve:

a few fingers of pitta bread (optional)

selection of soft vegetables for dipping, eg peeled cucumber or cooked beetroot, cut into sticks

This is fantastic for mums and dads as well as babies. Chickpeas are one of the most nutritionally valuable pulses, and a great source of protein for vegetarians, so tinned chickpeas are a useful store-cupboard ingredient. Do not serve tahini to babies if there is any family history of allergies.

1 Preheat oven to 190°C/375°F/gas mark 5.
2 Score a cross in each sweet potato and bake until they are soft and tender (approximately 40 minutes).
3 Scoop the potato flesh into a food processor, discarding the skins. Add the chickpeas, tahini, and garlic and whiz together. Add the lemon juice and enough oil to make the desired consistency.
4 Serve with toasted fingers of pitta bread, if using, and vegetable sticks.

bacon and mushrooms in cheese

makes : 4 baby portions or 2 baby portions and 1–2 adult portions

storage: 24 hours in the refrigerator

4 Portobello mushrooms

2 rashers unsmoked back bacon

1 tbsp olive oil

3 plum tomatoes

4 tbsp full-fat cream cheese

2 tbsp finely chopped flat-leaf parsley (or other herbs of your choice),

freshly ground black pepper

2 tbsp breadcrumbs

2 tbsp unsalted butter, melted

Vitamin B₁, A

This dish is easy to make and tastes delicious. This would also make a good supper dish for an adult, especially if served with a baked potato.

1 Preheat oven to 180°C/350°F/gas mark 4.

2 Remove the stalks from the mushrooms and finely chop them. Fry the bacon in a little oil in a frying pan until crisp, golden, and cooked through. Cut it into very small pieces and put into a bowl.

3 Add a little more oil to the pan and, when hot, add the mushroom stalks. Cook for a few minutes.

4 Chop the tomatoes, add to the bacon with the cooked mushroom stalks, cream cheese, herbs, and freshly ground black pepper.

5 Place the mushroom caps on a baking sheet. Spread the cream cheese mixture onto the mushrooms, then sprinkle over the breadcrumbs. Drizzle with butter and cook in the preheated oven for 10-15 minutes.

leek and ham mash

makes: 3 baby portions or 1 baby portion and 1 adult portion

storage: best eaten immediately

10g unsalted butter

2 small leeks, washed and finely chopped

2 medium potatoes, peeled and cut into 4

6 tbsp full-fat milk or calcium-enriched soya drink

2 slices cooked ham, finely diced

Vitamin B₁

A friend of mine, Lou, swears that she can get her children to eat any vegetables by mixing them with mashed potato. It's a good trick but hopefully your children will have got into the veg habit early on – especially if you are careful not to give them the idea that sweet things are nicer than vegetables.

1 Heat the butter in a heavy-based frying pan and fry the leeks until soft and pale golden (approximately 3-5 minutes).

2 Bring a pan of water to the boil and cook the potatoes until tender (approximately 10-12 minutes). Drain.

3 Add the milk to the potatoes and mash, then add the leeks and ham and mash again briefly.

quick bites lunches

things with pasta or noodles

Bring a large pan of water to the boil. Add 75g noodles or small pasta shapes and cook following the packet's instructions until just tender. Drain.

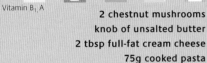

Vitamin B₁

½ | 2½ | 1½ | 18

2 tbsp smooth peanut butter
½ cooked chicken breast, finely chopped
75g cooked noodles

peanut noodles

Add the smooth peanut butter and cooked chicken to the noodles, then toss. Finely chop. Do not feed nut products to babies if there is a family history of allergies.

Vitamin B₁, A

½ | 1 | 1 | 6½

2 chestnut mushrooms
knob of unsalted butter
2 tbsp full-fat cream cheese
75g cooked pasta

cheese and mushroom pasta

Finely chop the chestnut mushrooms and fry them in the butter until soft. Add the cream cheese and the cooked pasta, then mix all the ingredients together. Finely chop.

Vitamin B₁, B₁₂, A

4 | 3½ | 1 | 21

50g Cheddar cheese
2 rashers unsmoked back bacon
75g cooked pasta

cheese and bacon pasta

Grate the Cheddar cheese and grill the bacon rashers until they are cooked and slightly crisp. Finely chop the bacon and stir into the pasta with the cheese. Finely chop.

4 | 2½ | 1½ | 23

50g Cheddar cheese
50g tinned tuna in oil, drained
75g cooked pasta

tuna pasta

Grate the Cheddar cheese. Add the tuna and grated cheese to the pasta, then toss everything together and mash slightly.

Vitamin B₁

4 | C | 1 | 1 | 7

a handful of cooked peas
2 tsp pesto
75g cooked noodles

pesto and peas

Simply mix together the cooked peas and pesto and then stir the mixture into the cooked noodles. Finely chop.

things with mashed potato

Bring a large pan of water to the boil. Peel and chop 1 medium potato or 1 sweet potato and cook until just tender (approximately 10–12 minutes). Drain, then mash with approximately 2 tbsp breast milk, formula milk or full-fat cow's milk.

sweetcorn and ham

Vitamin B₁ 2 C 1½ ½ 6

a handful of cooked sweetcorn
1 slice cooked ham, finely chopped
1 portion mash (recipe above)

Mix the cooked sweetcorn and finely chopped ham into the mash and heat through gently for 2 minutes.

pesto and pea mash

Vitamin B₁ 2½ C 1 1 4

2 tsp pesto
a handful of cooked peas
1 portion mash (recipe above)

Mix the pesto and the cooked peas into the mashed potatoes and lightly mash again.

cheese and onion mash

2 C 2 1½ ½ 8

1 tsp olive oil or unsalted butter
½ medium onion, finely chopped
2 tsp Cheddar cheese, grated
1 portion mash (recipe above)

Heat the olive oil or unsalted butter in a frying pan and sauté the onion until it is really soft (approximately 5 minutes). Add the onion to the mash with the grated Cheddar cheese and mix together.

tuna and tomato mash

Vitamin B₁, B₁₂, A 3 C 1 1 12

50g tuna tinned in oil, drained
1 ripe tomato, finely chopped
1 portion mash (recipe above)

Mix the tuna and finely chopped tomato into the mash, then lightly mash the mixture again.

things with rice

Mix 50g baby rice with breast milk or formula milk or full-fat cow's milk to achieve the desired consistency. Alternatively, mash 50g boiled basmati rice.

beetroot and spring onion

1 C ½ ½ ½ 2

1 tsp olive oil or unsalted butter
1 spring onion, finely sliced
1 small cooked beetroot, finely chopped
1 portion rice (recipe above)

Heat the olive oil or unsalted butter. Add the spring onion and sauté until really soft (3-4 minutes). Add the beetroot and mix with the rice, then lightly mash with a fork or potato masher.

broccoli and chicken

3 C ½ 1½ ½ 12

1 broccoli floret
1 portion rice (recipe above)
¼ cooked chicken breast, finely chopped

Bring a small pan of water to the boil. Add 1 broccoli floret and cook until just tender (about 3 minutes). Finely chop the broccoli and add to the rice with the chopped cooked chicken breast, then lightly mash.

All quick bites make 1 portion
unless otherwise stated.

lunches **to freeze**

chickpea and bacon stew

makes: 7–8 baby portions

storage: up to 2 months in the freezer

1 tbsp olive oil

130g pancetta or unsmoked
    back bacon, in small pieces

1 red onion, peeled, chopped

1 leek, washed and chopped

1 carrot, peeled and chopped

2 garlic cloves, peeled,
    chopped

Vitamin B₁, A

2 ripe tomatoes, chopped

400g tin tomatoes

400g tin chickpeas, drained
    and rinsed

450ml no-salt vegetable stock

1 tbsp fresh parsley, chopped

sprig of fresh rosemary

Introduce pulses gradually, or else they can be a little overwhelming for a baby's immature digestive system. Pulses are notorious for their "windiness", but as long as they are well-cooked, you should have no problems. Interestingly, parsley can help to counteract this side-effect, which is why I have added a little to this recipe.

1 Heat the oil in a heavy-based saucepan. Fry the pancetta or bacon until crisp, golden, and cooked through. Using a slotted spoon, transfer the meat to a plate.

2 In the same pan, sauté the onion, leek, carrot and garlic until they are soft (approximately 5-6 minutes).

3 Add the tomatoes and chickpeas and simmer for 5 minutes.

4 Add the stock, rosemary, parsley, and pancetta or bacon, then simmer for another 30 minutes.

5 Leave to cool, then spoon into a freeze-proof container or small freezer bags and freeze.

6 To serve, thaw thoroughly, remove the rosemary, and then roughly purée and heat through.

cheese and corn muffins

makes: 15 baby portions

storage: up to 3 months in the freezer

100g tinned sweetcorn

150g plain flour

½ tsp baking powder

1 large free-range egg

125ml full-fat milk

50g unsalted butter, melted

50g Cheddar cheese, grated

pinch of mild chilli powder

1 tbsp fresh parsley, chopped

These muffins are popular with children of all ages. Serve them with cheese and chopped tomato and avocado. They are also good served with soup.

1 Preheat the oven to 200°C/400°F/gas mark 6. Grease a mini-muffin tin or line with paper cases. Drain and mash the sweetcorn.

2 Sift the flour and baking powder into a large bowl. In another large bowl, mix together the egg, milk, melted butter, cheese, sweetcorn, chilli, and parsley.

3 Pour the flour mixture over the wet ingredients and quickly fold in. Don't overmix, as it should look lumpy. Spoon into the tin and bake for 15 minutes until risen and golden. Cool on a wire rack and freeze in a freezerproof container.

4 To serve, heat through from frozen in a preheated oven at 180°C/350°F/gas mark 4 for 5-6 minutes. Break into very small pieces.

mild curried parsnip and pear soup

makes: 10 baby portions

storage: up to 3 months in the freezer

1 tbsp olive oil

25g unsalted butter

1 small onion, peeled and chopped

1 garlic clove, peeled and chopped

1 medium potato, peeled and chopped

600g parsnips, peeled, chopped

1 tsp mild curry powder

1 litre water

1 ripe pear, peeled, cored, and chopped

300ml full-fat milk, to serve

My whole family loves this soup – the pears work really well and the curry powder brings out the parsnip flavour. Try serving it with some warm, Indian-style bread, such as naan, which is soft and easy for babies to chew. This is quite a thick soup, which should make it slightly easier for your baby to eat without making too much of a mess.

1 Heat the oil and butter in a heavy-based saucepan.
2 Fry the onion and garlic until soft, then add the potato, parsnips, and curry powder and cook for a further 1-2 minutes. Stir the mixture to prevent it sticking to the pan.
3 Add the water and pear and bring up to the boil. Simmer gently for 20 minutes, until the parsnips are soft.
4 Blend with a hand-held blender (or in a food processor or blender) until really smooth.
5 Freeze in a freezerproof container or freezer bags.
6 To serve, thaw thoroughly, add the milk, and reheat gently in a saucepan without boiling.

fruity moroccan lamb burgers

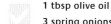

makes: 20 baby portions

storage: up to 2 months in the freezer

Vitamin B₁₂

1 tbsp olive oil

3 spring onions, finely chopped

pinch of ground coriander

500g lean minced lamb

50g dried dates, finely chopped

1 tsp fresh coriander, chopped (optional)

These burgers can be fried, grilled or cooked in the oven. If you are grilling them, be careful not to let the edges burn. Giving babies any food that has very dark or crispy edges, such as chargrilled or barbecued food, should be avoided.

1 If oven cooking, preheat the oven to 200°C/400°F/gas mark 6.
2 Heat the oil in a heavy-based frying pan and fry the onions until just soft (approximately 5 minutes). Add the ground coriander and cook for a further 2 minutes, stirring often.
3 Transfer the onions to a bowl, then add the lamb, dates, and coriander and mix together well with your hands.
4 Mould the mixture into about 20 little burgers. Wrap in foil and freeze.
5 To serve, thaw thoroughly. Preheat the grill to high. Grill the burgers for 5 minutes on each side until cooked through. Test if the burgers are cooked by inserting a skewer into the middle of the burger – the juices should run absolutely clear.

fish and courgette gratin

17½

½

1½

3

1

Vitamin B₁,B₁₂, A

1+

makes: 4 baby portions

storage: up to 2 months in the freezer

25g unsalted butter
25g plain flour
600ml full-fat milk
pinch of freshly grated nutmeg
freshly ground black pepper
100g pasta shells or twists
2 medium courgettes, thinly
   sliced
450g white fish, skinned,
   boned and cut into small
   pieces
150g Cheddar cheese, grated

White fish is a brilliant food for babies – it's a great source of protein, but is relatively easy for them to digest. This is a delicious cheesy gratin that is suitable for all the family. All you need to serve with it is some green vegetables, such as spinach or broccoli.

1 Preheat the oven to 180°C/350°F/gas mark 4. Make an all-in-one sauce by putting the butter, flour, and milk into a saucepan. Heat gently, stirring constantly until the sauce thickens. You may like to use a whisk to prevent any lumps from forming. Add the nutmeg and a little freshly ground back pepper.

2 Bring a large pan of water to the boil and cook the pasta following the packet's instructions. Put the courgettes into a steamer and cook over the pasta for a few minutes until just tender.

3 Put the fish and courgettes into a gratin dish. Add the pasta and mix everything together. Cover with the sauce, then scatter over the cheese. Bake at 180°C/350°F/gas mark 4 for 20-25 minutes. Leave to cool, wrap up in foil, and freeze.

4 Thaw thoroughly. Preheat the oven to 180°C/350°F/gas mark 4. Cook for 15-20 minutes, until thoroughly heated through and golden on the top. Lightly mash.

stuffed baked potatoes

10

½

1

2

1

Vitamin B₁,B₁₂, A

1+

makes: 2 baby portions

storage: up to 2 months in the freezer

1 medium potato
10g unsalted butter
50g tinned tuna in oil,
   drained and flaked
50g Cheddar cheese, grated
1 tsp fresh parsley, chopped
freshly ground black pepper

These are really quick and easy. Make and freeze a big batch of them for maximum convenience. There are lots of ingredients you can add to the fillings: sautéed mushrooms and parsley, spinach and cheese, ham and tomato or baked beans and cheese.

1 Preheat the oven to 180°C/350°F/gas mark 4. Bake the potato for 1 hour, until soft.

2 Remove from oven, carefully cut the potato in half, and scoop out the flesh. Mash the flesh in a bowl with the butter, tuna, half the cheese and the parsley. Season with black pepper.

3 Refill the potato skin and sprinkle with the remaining cheese. Freeze.

4 Thaw thoroughly. Bake on a baking sheet in a preheated oven at 180°C/350°F/gas mark 4 until the filling is hot and the cheese is golden brown and bubbling (approximately 15 minutes). Leave to cool slightly before serving and, if necessary, chop into very small pieces.

fresh suppers

chicken goujons

makes: 6 baby portions or 2 baby portion and 2 adult portions

storage: serve immediately

200ml natural full-fat yogurt
2 tbsp fresh herbs,
  eg parsley, basil, sage,
  finely chopped
2 raw chicken breasts, cut
  into thin strips 1.5cm thick
freshly ground black pepper
75g fine fresh breadcrumbs
large pinch of paprika
olive oil, to drizzle

Sadly, chicken nuggets, one of the most popular foods among kids, are often packed with some of the worst ingredients for small children (or adults for that matter). They can be notoriously high in additives and made from poor quality meat. It may take a little more effort to make your own, but it will be worth it in the long run. Only serve this to babies who are very confident with chewing.

1 Preheat the oven to 180°C/350°F/gas mark 4.
2 Mix the yogurt and herbs together and divide in two.
3 Stir the chicken into half the yogurt, making sure the meat is all coated. Leave to marinade for at least an hour, or overnight in the refrigerator if possible.
4 Season the remaining half of the yogurt mixture with black pepper, then cover and keep as a dip for the goujons.
5 Grease a baking sheet. Mix the breadcrumbs with the paprika and black pepper. Dip each goujon into the breadcrumb mixture and lay on the baking sheet.
6 Drizzle with olive oil and cook for 20-25 minutes, until the goujons are golden and cooked through.

baked bean gratin

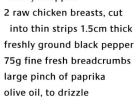

makes: 2 baby portions

storage: best eaten immediately

1 large potato, peeled, halved
2 good-quality low salt pork
  sausages, cooked
420g tin baked beans,
  preferably sugar-free
50g Cheddar cheese, grated

Vitamin B₁, B₁₂

Note: babies develop at different rates; do not feed chopped food to your baby until he is confident with chewing.

There are lots of convenience foods that make life with children much easier. However, it's best not to rely on them and, if you do use them, make sure you cook or serve them with fresh vegetables or fruits as appropriate.

1 Bring a pan of water to the boil and cook the potato until tender (approximately 10 minutes). Drain. Preheat the oven to 180°C/350°F/gas mark 4.
2 Cut the cooked sausages into very small bite-size pieces – if they are too big there is a danger of choking.
3 Pour the baked beans into a gratin dish. Sprinkle over the sausage pieces.
4 Slice the potato halves and lay over the sausage and beans. Sprinkle with the cheese and bake in the oven for 20 minutes, until the top is golden and bubbling and it is hot all the way through. Lightly mash before serving.

chicken and potato cakes

8

½

1

½

½ C

Vitamin B₁₂

1+

makes: 10 baby portions

storage: keep covered in the refrigerator for up to 48 hours

2 large free-range eggs, beaten

200ml full-fat milk

125g plain flour

450g potatoes or sweet potatoes, peeled and coarsely grated

1 large onion, thinly sliced

2 cooked chicken breasts, finely chopped

200g tinned sweetcorn, drained

freshly ground black pepper

1 tbsp fresh coriander, chopped

This variation on fish cakes is really popular in my household. If you fancy eating some of these yourself, you may like to dip them into a little soy and/or sweet chilli sauce.

1 Whisk the eggs and milk together, then beat in the flour thoroughly to make a smooth batter.
2 Bring a small pan of water to the boil. Add the potatoes and onion and blanch for 2-3 minutes, then drain well, pressing out as much liquid as possible.
3 Stir the chicken into the batter with the sweetcorn, potato and onion, black pepper, and coriander.
4 Rub a heavy-based frying pan with an oiled kitchen towel and heat. Drop rounded teaspoons of batter into the pan (or dessertspoons, if you want larger cakes), flatten a little with a spatula and cook for 2 minutes on each side until golden if they are small, and 3-4 minutes each side if larger.
5 Keep warm, uncovered, in an oven at 150°C/300°F/gas mark 3. Repeat until the mixture is used up. Serve warm, broken into small pieces.

eastern rice with baby veg

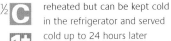

2

½

½ C

1+

makes: 4 baby portions or 2 baby portions and 2 adult portions

storage: rice should not be reheated but can be kept cold in the refrigerator and served cold up to 24 hours later

3 mange-tout

3 baby carrots

3 baby corn

200g basmati rice

400ml water

10g creamed coconut, crumbled

4 cardamon pods

1 cinnamon stick

squeeze of lime juice

handful of chopped fresh coriander, (optional)

You and your partner might enjoy this dish served with grilled chicken or steamed fish. Do not serve coconut to babies if there is any family history of allergies.

1 Thinly slice the mange-tout, baby carrots, and baby corn into even-size pieces to make sure that they cook evenly.
2 Put the rice, water, creamed coconut, cardamon pods, and cinnamon stick into a saucepan, stir well, then cover and bring up to simmering point. Simmer for 11 minutes without removing the lid.
3 Remove the pan from the heat. Throw the sliced vegetables on top of the rice and quickly replace the lid, then cook for another 14 minutes.
4 Remove the cardamom pods and cinnamon stick. Add the lime juice, toss everything together and scatter in a little fresh coriander, if using. Mash if necessary.

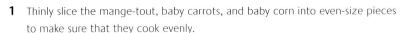

lamb chops with pea mash

makes: 5 baby portions or 1 baby portion and 2 adult portions

storage: best eaten immediately

450g potatoes, peeled and roughly chopped

150g frozen peas or petits pois

15g knob of unsalted butter

100ml full-fat milk

5 lamb chops

mint sauce, to serve (optional)

14

2

4

½

2

Vitamin B₁, B₁₂

1⁺

Flavoured mash is really popular with my children, especially this pea one, because it is lovely and sweet. If you like, add a little chopped fresh mint, or a tiny bit of mint sauce to the mash. Cook as many lamb chops as you need. I have suggested five, as you can cook one for the baby and two each for you and your partner.

1 Bring a large pan of water to the boil. Add the potatoes and cook until just tender (approximately 10 minutes). Just before they are cooked, add the peas and bring back to the boil. Drain. Add the butter and milk and, using a potato masher, mash together.

2 Cook the lamb chops under a hot grill for 4-5 minutes on each side.

3 Chop one lamb chop into small pieces and serve with some mash and a little mint sauce, if using.

savoury crumble

makes: 5 baby portions or 1 baby portion and 2 adult portions

storage: up to 24 hours in the refrigerator

25g unsalted butter

25g plain flour

300ml full-fat milk

freshly grated nutmeg

freshly ground black pepper

75g broccoli or cauliflower

75g carrots, peeled

150g cooked chicken

75g frozen peas

1 tbsp finely chopped fresh parsley

for the crumble:

50g strong Cheddar cheese, grated

2 tbsp fresh herbs, chopped

40g fresh breadcrumbs

40g nuts, ground

12

1

1½

2

3½

Vitamin B₁₂, A

1⁺

You could just as easily use tinned tuna instead of the chicken or, for a vegetarian meal, just add cooked quorn or tofu instead. If you have any cold leftover vegetables use those, too. As with sweet crumble, it's great to have a bag of this topping made up and kept in the freezer. Remember, only serve nuts to babies if there is no family history of allergies.

1 Preheat the oven to 180°C/350°F/gas mark 4.

2 Make an all-in-one sauce by putting the butter, flour, and milk into a saucepan. Heat gently, stirring constantly, until the sauce thickens. You may like to use a whisk to prevent from lumps from forming. Add the nutmeg and a little black pepper.

3 Cut the broccoli or cauliflower and carrots into small pieces. Also cut the chicken into bite-sized chunks.

4 Bring a large pan of water to the boil. Cook the broccoli or cauliflower and carrots until they are just tender, then drain.

5 Gently stir the cooked vegetables, peas, chicken, and parsley into the sauce and pour into a gratin dish.

6 To make the crumble, mix together all the ingredients. Scatter over the chicken and vegetables.

7 Bake in the preheated oven for 30 minutes until cooked through and golden on the top. Finely chop or mash before serving.

leek and chive macaroni cheese

6

½

1

2

½

Vitamin B₁₂, A

makes: 4 baby portions or 2 baby portions and 1 adult portion

storage: up to 24 hours in the refrigerator

100g macaroni pasta
1 tbsp olive oil
1 medium leek, cleaned and sliced
200ml full-fat milk or calcium-enriched soya drink
20g plain flour
20g unsalted butter
freshly ground black pepper
2 tbsp fresh chives, finely chopped
100g Cheddar cheese, grated

Macaroni cheese is a great family staple, and you can add pretty much anything you like to make it more interesting: leftover cooked vegetables, crumbled cooked bacon, chopped cooked ham or tomatoes or flaked tinned tuna. Use a medium-strength Cheddar rather than mild to make sure that your finished dish has a decent flavour.

1 Bring a pan of water to the boil and cook the macaroni following the packet's instructions. Drain.
2 Heat the oil in a heavy-based frying pan and sauté the leeks until soft (approximately 6-8 minutes).
3 Preheat the oven to 180°C/350°F/gas mark 4.
4 Mix together the milk, flour, and butter in a saucepan. Heat gently, stirring constantly with a whisk, until you have a smooth sauce.
5 Season with black pepper and add the chives. Add half the cheese and stir until it has melted. Stir in the cooked macaroni and leeks.
6 Pour into an ovenproof dish and sprinkle over the remaining cheese. Bake for 15-20 minutes, until bubbling and golden brown on top.
7 Chop into tiny pieces or lightly mash before serving.

green bean and tuna gratin

11

1

1½

2

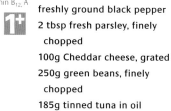
Vitamin B₁₂, A

makes: 7 baby portions or 1 baby portion and 3 adult portions

storage: up to 24 hours in the refrigerator

600ml full-fat milk or calcium-enriched soya drink
25g plain flour
25g unsalted butter
freshly ground black pepper
2 tbsp fresh parsley, finely chopped
100g Cheddar cheese, grated
250g green beans, finely chopped
185g tinned tuna in oil
200g pasta shapes, cooked and drained

You can use either tinned tuna or tinned salmon in this gratin – whichever you prefer.

1 Preheat the oven to 180°C/350°F/gas mark 4.
2 Mix together the milk, flour and butter in a saucepan. Heat gently, stirring constantly with a whisk, until you have a smooth sauce.
3 Season with black pepper, then add the parsley. Add half the cheese and stir until it has melted.
4 Bring a pan of water to the boil and cook the beans until just tender – approximately 3-4 minutes. Drain. Drain and flake the tuna.
5 Stir the tuna, green beans and cooked pasta into the sauce and pour into a lightly buttered ovenproof dish. Sprinkle over the remaining cheese.
6 Bake in the oven for 20-25 minutes until the sauce is bubbling and the top is golden brown. Mash slightly with a fork before serving.

mushroom and bacon ragout

makes: 4 baby portions or 2 baby portion and 2 adult portions

storage: up to 24 hours in the refrigerator

1 tbsp olive oil

4 rashers unsmoked streaky bacon, in small pieces

1 small onion, peeled and finely chopped

1 garlic clove, peeled and finely chopped

350g mushrooms, cut into very small pieces

2 tsp tomato purée

100ml no-salt vegetable stock

large sprig fresh rosemary

250ml tomato passata

freshly ground black pepper

mashed potato, to serve

Vitamin B₁

When you are buying garlic, always look for plump, unbruised bulbs with no sprouts as these will be the freshest. Be careful not to over-brown the garlic when cooking it, because it will add an unpleasant and bitter flavour to your dish.

1 Heat the oil in a heavy-based pan and then fry the bacon until it is crisp, golden, and cooked through. Remove the bacon with a slotted spoon and reserve.

2 Add the chopped onion to the pan, cover, and sweat it slowly without colouring, for 5-10 minutes. Add the garlic and cook for a further 2 minutes.

3 Add the mushrooms and cook over a medium heat for 5 minutes, stirring often.

4 Add the tomato purée, stock, rosemary, and cooked bacon. Turn the heat down and cook for 10 minutes.

5 Add the tomato passata, and black pepper to taste and then cook the mixture for a further 10 minutes. Lightly mash before serving with mashed potato.

moroccan beef

makes: 4 baby portions or 2 baby portions and 2 adult portions

storage: 48 hours in the refrigerator

1 tbsp olive oil

450g beef mince, finely chopped

1 large onion, peeled, chopped

1 cloves garlic, peeled and finely chopped

100g dried apricots, finely chopped

75g sultanas

pinch of ground cinnamon

400ml tomato passata

200ml water

couscous, rice or pasta, to serve

Vitamin B₁,B₁₂

The classic Moroccan combination of fruit, meat, and mild spices is always popular with babies. You can make this with lamb mince or finely chopped chicken instead of beef mince; just adapt the cooking time accordingly. Serve with couscous, rice or pasta.

1 Heat a large, heavy-based frying pan until really hot. Add half of the oil and then the beef. Fry until browned all over. Transfer to a plate.

2 Heat the remaining oil in a small, heavy-based frying pan and sauté the onion and garlic until soft and pale golden.

3 Add the apricots, sultanas, cinnamon, tomato passata, beef, and water. Bring to the boil, cover and simmer gently for 30 minutes.

4 Cook the couscous, rice or pasta according to the packet instructions and serve with the Moroccan beef stew. Lightly mash before serving.

quick bites suppers

carrot and courgette pasta

1 small carrot, peeled and grated
½ medium courgette, grated
small knob of unsalted butter
2 tbsp full-fat cream cheese
75g pasta, freshly cooked

Fry the carrot and courgettes in the butter until tender. Stir in the cream cheese and heat gently until it has melted. Pour over the pasta and finely chop or lightly mash before serving.

sweetcorn and cheese pasta

small knob of unsalted butter
75g tinned sweetcorn
30g Cheddar cheese, grated
1 tsp fresh parsley, finely chopped
75g pasta, freshly cooked

Heat the butter in a pan and add the sweetcorn. Heat through, then add the rest of the ingredients and mix together well. Finely chop or lightly mash before serving.

ham and pea pasta

75g frozen peas
75g pasta, freshly cooked
1 tsp finely chopped fresh parsley
½ slice cooked ham, finely chopped

Mix the peas, pasta and parsley together in a saucepan and heat gently. When heated through. If you wish, add a little full-fat cream cheese or tomato passata to make more of a sauce. Remove from the heat and stir in the finely chopped cooked ham. Finely chop or lightly mash before serving.

     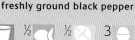

creamy spinach pasta sauce

75g green pasta, freshly cooked
75g fresh spinach, chopped and cooked
2 tbsp full-fat cream cheese
pinch of grated nutmeg
freshly ground black pepper

Mix the pasta, spinach and cream cheese together in a pan and heat gently until heated through. Add the nutmeg and a pinch of finely ground black pepper. Finely chop or lightly mash before serving.

tortelloni with buttered breadcrumbs

75g tortelloni
small knob of unsalted butter
30g fresh breadcrumbs
1 tsp finely chopped fresh parsley
freshly ground black pepper

Cook the pasta following the packet's instructions. Drain. Meanwhile, melt the butter in a pan and fry the breadcrumbs until golden. Add the cooked pasta and parsley. Stir gently and season with black pepper. Finely chop or lightly mash before serving.

tomato baked beans on toast

1 C ½ 🥛 1 🐟 1½ 🍃 5 🥚

75g baked beans
1 tomato, finely chopped
1 slice wholemeal bread

Heat the beans in a pan with the tomato until hot. Toast the bread and serve with the beans. Cut into small pieces.

baked beans with sausage

✓ ½ 🥛 ½ 🐟 1 🍃 4½ 🥚

Vitamin B₁₂

1 good-quality low-salt pork sausage
75g baked beans

Cook the sausage under a grill so that the fat drains away. Meanwhile, heat the beans until warmed right through. When the sausage is cooked through, chop it finely and stir it into the beans. If you can, buy sausages made with herbs or leeks to make this more tasty. If necessary, lightly mash before serving.

baked beans with tuna and cheese

✓ 1½ 🥛 1 🐟 1 🍃 10½ 🥚

Vitamin B₁₂

75g baked beans
30g tinned tuna in oil, drained and flaked
15g Cheddar cheese, grated

Heat the beans with the tuna in a small pan. When they are just simmering, stir in the cheese. If necessary, lightly mash before serving.

spaghetti with mushrooms

½ 🐟 ½ 🍃 1½ 🥚

50g mushrooms, finely chopped
dash of olive oil
75g tinned spaghetti in tomato sauce

Fry the mushrooms in the olive oil. When they are golden, add the spaghetti and cook until heated through. If necessary, lightly mash before serving.

spaghetti with sweetcorn

1 C ½ 🍃 2 🥚

75g tinned spaghetti in tomato sauce
50g tinned sweetcorn

Heat the spaghetti and stir in the sweetcorn, then cook until heated through. Lightly mash before serving if necessary.

fish baked in orange juice

✓ 3 C ½ 🐟 9½ 🥚

Vitamin B₁₂

75g piece raw white fish, skinned and boned
4 tbsp fresh orange juice
bread and butter or mashed potato, to serve

Put the fish into a baking dish with the orange juice. Cover with foil and bake in an oven at 180°C/350°F/gas mark 4 until cooked through (approximately 5-10 minutes). Finely chop or lightly mash before serving with a piece of bread and unsalted butter or mashed potato.

mexican couscous

✓ ½ C 1 🐟 1 🍃 10½ 🥚

Vitamin B₁

50g couscous, cooked
50g cold cooked chicken, finely chopped
¼ ripe avocado, peeled and finely chopped
lemon juice (optional)
fresh coriander, finely chopped (optional)

Mix together the cooked couscous, cooked chicken and avocado, adding a little lemon juice and coriander if you have them to hand. If necessary, lightly mash before serving.

All quick bites make 1 portion unless otherwise stated.

suppers to freeze

sausage, apple and parsnip pie

8½

1½

1½

2

3

Vitamin B₁, B₁₂

1+

makes: 4 baby portions

storage: up to 2 months in the freezer

4 good-quality low-salt pork sausages

2 medium potatoes, peeled and halved

1 tbsp olive oil

1 small onion, peeled and finely chopped

1 garlic clove, peeled, crushed

1 leek, cleaned and sliced

2 parsnips, peeled and diced

2 eating apples, peeled, cored and sliced

1 tbsp parsley, finely chopped

150ml no-salt veg stock

50ml apple juice

50g Cheddar cheese, grated

Choose sausages with a high meat content – at least 80 per cent meat. This dish makes a great family supper and freezes well.

1 Heat the oven to 200°C/400°F/gas mark 6. Put the sausages on a baking tray and cook for 20 minutes, turning occasionally, until cooked through and golden all over. Cook the potatoes in boiling water until just tender (approximately 10-15 minutes). Drain and slice thinly.

2 Meanwhile, heat the oil in a heavy-based frying pan and fry the onion and garlic until soft. Add the leek, parsnips, and apples and cook for a further 15 minutes, stirring often. Add the parsley, stock, and apple juice and 100ml boiling water and bring to the boil.

3 Slice the sausages and scatter over the bottom of an ovenproof dish. Pour over the vegetable mixture and top with the potato slices. Leave to cool.

4 Wrap in foil and freeze. To serve, thaw thoroughly. Cover with foil and bake for 35 minutes at 200°C/400°F/gas mark 6. Remove the foil, sprinkle with cheese, and bake for a further 20 minutes. If necessary, finely chop or mash before serving.

sweet potato and coconut gratin

1

1

Vitamin A

1+

makes: 15 baby portions

storage: up to 3 months in the freezer

600g potatoes, peeled

250g sweet potatoes, peeled and very thinly sliced

3 spring onions, finely sliced

2 tsp mild curry powder

400ml coconut milk

2 tbsp coriander, finely chopped

Note: do not feed chopped food to your baby until he is confident with chewing.

This is a delicious dish, but do not serve coconut to babies if there is any family history of allergies

1 Preheat the oven to 180°C/350°F/gas mark 4. Bring a pan of water to the boil, add the ordinary potatoes, and parboil for 5 minutes. Drain and slice thinly.

2 Layer some of both types of potato into the bottom of a buttered ovenproof dish. Scatter some of the spring onions over the top and sprinkle with a little of the curry powder. Repeat until all of the potatoes have been used up.

3 Mix the coconut milk and 150-200ml water together, then pour onto the potatoes. Bake for 40-50 minutes, until the potatoes are tender. Scatter over the coriander and finely chop or mash before serving. Alternatively, leave to cool, wrap in foil and freeze. Thaw thoroughly, then reheat for 20-30 minutes at 180°C/350°F/gas mark 4 until hot right through, then finely chop or mash.

home-made fish fingers

makes: 3 baby portions

storage: up to 2 months in the freezer

Vitamin B₁₂

300g fresh cod fillet, skin and bones removed and cooked

approx 3 tbsp plain flour, for dusting

pinch of freshly ground black pepper

pinch of paprika

1 large free-range egg, beaten

75g breadcrumbs

vegetable oil, for frying

My girls love these more than the shop-bought variety and they take very little time or effort to make. Serve with a few peas or baked beans and a little mashed potato for a healthy and tasty supper.

1 Cut the cod into 2cm-wide strips and, if they are too long, cut these strips in half. Season the flour with a little black pepper and paprika. Dip the fish into the flour and shake off any excess.

2 Dip the seasoned fish into the beaten egg, then roll it in the breadcrumbs until it is evenly coated.

3 Layer with sheets of greaseproof paper in a freezerproof container and freeze.

4 To serve, leave to thaw thoroughly, resting on kitchen paper, then heat enough oil to cover the base of a large non-stick frying pan. Arrange the defrosted fish fingers in the pan (you may have to cook them in batches), and fry them over a medium heat for 3 to 4 minutes on each side until crisp and golden. Drain on kitchen paper and, if necessary, finely chop or mash before serving.

mini quiches

Vitamin B₁ B₁₂, A

makes: 6 baby portions

storage: up to 2 months in the freezer

for the pastry:

175g plain flour, sieved

90g unsalted butter, cut into small pieces and kept in the refrigerator

1 egg yolk plus 1 tbsp cold water, or 2–4 tbsp cold water

for the fillings:

15g unsalted butter

1 small onion, finely chopped

125g courgettes, thinly sliced

125g broccoli, in small pieces

50g Gruyère cheese, grated

2 large free-range eggs plus 1 extra free-range egg yolk

270ml full-fat milk

These can be made with lots of different fillings – use whatever you have to hand. Mini versions of things seems to go down really well with children.

1 Put the flour into a food processor and whiz for a minute to aerate. Add the butter and whiz until the mixture resembles fine breadcrumbs.

2 Add the egg yolk and cold water, if necessary, and whiz until the pastry draws together. Turn onto a floured surface and knead to form a flat round.

3 Use the pastry to line six chilled 10cm quiche tins, trim the edges, and chill for 1 hour. Preheat the oven to 190°C/375°F/gas mark 5. Cover the pastry cases with greaseproof paper and baking beans and bake blind for 5 minutes. Remove the paper and beans and cook until just light golden (about 5 minutes). Remove from the oven and reduce the heat.

4 For the filling, heat the butter in a frying pan and soften the onion for 5 minutes. Add the courgettes and brown a little, turning frequently. Spoon into the pastry cases with the broccoli and top with the grated cheese.

5 Beat the eggs and yolk, then whisk in the milk. Pour over the filling, place the quiches on a baking tray, and bake until the centres are set and the fillings are golden and puffy (20-25 minutes). Cool slightly, then serve. Alternatively, leave to cool, wrap in foil, and freeze. Thaw thoroughly, then bake at 180°C/350°F/gas mark 4 for 5 minutes. If necessary, finely chop or mash before serving.

chicken and mushroom broth

makes: 4 baby portions

storage: up to 3 months in the freezer

1 tbsp olive oil

200g raw chicken, breast or thigh, cut into chunks

1 large onion, peeled and chopped

2 medium carrots, peeled and chopped

150g chestnut mushroom, sliced

1 tbsp fresh herbs, eg rosemary, tarragon, parsley, finely chopped

1 tbsp tomato purée

500ml no-salt light veg stock

125g noodles, chopped

Vitamin B₁, A

Many of the recipes in this book use herbs. If you have bought fresh herbs for a recipe and find that you do not need them all, finely chop any left over herbs and put into ice-cube trays with a little water, then freeze. That way you won't waste them and you have handy herb cubes to add to other dishes.

1 Heat the oil in a casserole. Fry the chicken until just golden, remove with a slotted spoon, and reserve. Fry the onion and carrots until soft and translucent (approximately 5 minutes). Add the mushrooms and cook over a high heat stirring often until they begin to lose their juice.

2 Add the herbs, tomato purée, and vegetable stock, then return the chicken to the pan and bring to the boil. Simmer for 10 minutes, until the chicken is cooked.

3 Leave to cool. Freeze in a freezerproof container or in freezer bags.

4 To serve, thaw thoroughly and then reheat in a saucepan by simmering for at least 10 minutes, until piping hot. Add the noodles and cook for another 5 minutes. If necessary, finely chop or mash before serving.

veggie burgers

makes: 8 baby portions

storage: up to 2 months in the freezer

450g potatoes, peeled and cut into chunks

30g unsalted butter

200g cooked vegetables, eg carrots, courgettes, peas, leeks – all well drained

50g tinned butterbeans, rinsed, drained and mashed

2 tbsp fresh herbs, eg parsley, thyme, finely chopped

50g Cheddar cheese, grated

freshly ground black pepper

1 large free-range egg, beaten

90g dried breadcrumbs

vegetable oil, for frying

Vitamin B₁, B₁₂, A

Shop bought veggie burgers are often one of the most disappointing convenience foods. These are easy to make and freeze really well, so it's worth making a double batch.

1 Cook the potatoes in boiling water until tender (approximately 10 minutes). Drain and mash with the butter.

2 Stir in the cooked vegetables, mashed butterbeans, herbs, cheese, and pepper.

3 Using your hands (wet hands are probably easiest), form the mixture into approximately 16 balls and then flatten into patties.

4 Dip each patty in beaten egg and then into breadcrumbs, making sure each side is well-covered, then lay on a plate. Layer with greaseproof paper in a freezerproof container. Freeze.

5 To serve, thaw thoroughly on kitchen paper. Pour enough oil into a frying pan just to cover the bottom. Fry the patties over a medium heat until golden on both sides (approximately 6-8 minutes). Blot on kitchen paper and serve immediately. If necessary, finely chop or mash before serving.

piggies in blankets

makes: 12 baby portions

storage: up to 2 months in the freezer

225g self-raising flour
½ tsp baking powder
40g unsalted butter, plus
  extra for greasing
50g sun-dried tomatoes,
  finely chopped
25g fresh parsley, finely
  chopped
75g Cheddar cheese, grated
150ml full-fat milk
25 chipolata sausages,
  cooked and cooled

These are a great alternative to sausage rolls. You can add other ingredients to the scone mix if you prefer, such as fresh herbs or mustard. If you don't want to make lots of piggies in blankets, just use 10 sausages and make the rest of the scone mixture into little scones (see page 150), which you can freeze.

1 Grease a baking sheet with a little butter. Preheat the oven to 200°C/400°F/gas mark 6.
2 Sift the flour and baking powder into a bowl. Rub in the butter until the mixture resembles breadcrumbs.
3 Stir in the sun-dried tomatoes, parsley, and cheese. Make a well in the centre. Mix in enough milk to give a soft dough. On a lightly-floured surface, roll out the dough to 8mm thick.
4 Cut out 25 squares. Wrap a square of dough around each chipolata and use a little milk to stick down the edges.
5 Place on a baking sheet and brush the tops with milk. Bake for 8-10 minutes until risen and golden. Serve warm, finely chopped if necessary. Alternatively, leave to cool and freeze in freezer bags. Thaw thoroughly, then reheat in an oven at 180°C/350°F/gas mark 4 until warmed through (approximately 5-10 minutes).

chicken and sesame patties

makes: 4 baby portion

storage: up to 2 months in the freezer

Vitamin B₁

2 cooked chicken breasts,
  skin removed and roughly
  chopped
1 garlic clove, peeled and
  chopped
1 tbsp fresh basil, torn
dash sweet chilli sauce
  (optional)
freshly ground black pepper
40g sesame seeds, ground
vegetable oil, for frying

These are really delicious. Try serving them with some mashed avocado or guacamole (see page 112) and tomato salad. Do not serve seeds to babies if there is any family history of allergies.

1 Put the chicken, garlic, basil, a dash of sweet chilli sauce (if using), and black pepper into a food processor and whiz until smooth.
2 Take large teaspoons of the mixture and, with wet hands, roll into balls. Roll the balls in the sesame seeds, flatten slightly and put on a plate.
3 Layer with sheets of greaseproof paper in a freezerproof container. Freeze.
4 To serve, thaw thoroughly on kitchen paper. Pour enough oil into a frying pan to just cover the bottom and heat. Fry the patties over a medium heat until golden on both sides (approximately 8–10 minutes), drain on kitchen paper, and finely chop or mash before serving.

cottage pie

makes: 4 baby portions or 2 baby portions and 1 adult portion

storage: up to 2 months in the freezer

2 tbsp olive oil
250g lean beef mince
1 medium leek, chopped
2 carrots, peeled and diced
1 garlic clove, peeled, crushed
100g button mushrooms, sliced
200g tinned kidney beans
400g tin chopped tomatoes
2 tbsp fresh herbs, chopped
5 medium potatoes, peeled and chopped in half
knob unsalted butter
3–4 tbsp full-fat milk, plus extra for glazing
freshly ground black pepper

Vitamin B₁₂,B₁₂, A

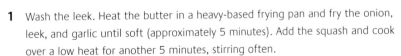

This is a brilliant freezer stand-by for all the family. If you prefer, make smaller cottage pies, which are more convenient for defrosting if you are just feeding one baby. Ramekins are ideal for this, but you will need to reduce the final cooking time to between 20-25 minutes. If you have any extra fresh herbs, such as parsley, add some to the mash.

1 Heat 1 tbsp of oil in a frying pan and fry the mince until browned. Reserve.
2 Wash the leek. Heat the remaining oil and fry the leek and carrots until soft and pale golden (approximately 5 minutes). Add the garlic and mushrooms and fry for another 5 minutes, stirring often.
3 Add the kidney beans, tomatoes and herbs, then stir well. Add 200ml water and return the mince to the pan. Season with black pepper, bring to the boil and simmer gently for 35 minutes until the mince is cooked and the sauce is thick.
5 Meanwhile, cook the potatoes in boiling water until tender (approximately 10 minutes). Drain and mash with the milk and butter. Put the mince into a baking dish and top with the mashed potato. Rough the top with a fork and brush with a little milk. Cool before wrapping with foil or clingfilm and freezing.
6 To serve, thaw thoroughly. Cook at 180°C/350°F/gas mark 4 for 30-35 minutes, until the top is golden and crunchy. If necessary, finely chop or mash.

squash and gruyère gratin

makes 4 baby portions

storage up to two months in freezer

1 small leek, finely sliced
25g unsalted butter
1 small onion, finely chopped
1 garlic clove, peeled, crushed
500g butternut squash flesh, peeled and in small cubes
200ml tomato passata
200ml water or no-salt vegetable stock
4 tbsp natural Greek yogurt
knob of unsalted butter
100g breadcrumbs
100g Gruyère cheese, grated

Vitamin B₁₂,B₁₂, A

This is a yummy winter dish. Adults will enjoy this as a lunch on its own or as an accompaniment to something more substantial, such as a chicken or pork roast. If you have any sage growing in your garden, a little would be a great addition to this dish.

1 Wash the leek. Heat the butter in a heavy-based frying pan and fry the onion, leek, and garlic until soft (approximately 5 minutes). Add the squash and cook over a low heat for another 5 minutes, stirring often.
2 Add the tomato passata and water or stock, then simmer for 10-15 minutes, until the squash is just soft. Stir in the yogurt and black pepper.
3 Pour into a buttered ovenproof dish. Melt the knob of butter in a pan, add the breadcrumbs and stir well. Sprinkle the buttery breadcrumbs and grated cheese over the top of the squash mixture.
4 Leave to cool, then wrap with foil or cling film and freeze. Thaw thoroughly. Bake at 180°C/350°F/gas mark 4 for 40 minutes, until the top is crisp and golden. Finely chop or mash before serving.

quick bites finger foods

 apple and raisin toast

1 tbsp thick apple purée (see page 78)
1 piece raisin bread, toasted

Thick apple purée is great to spread on bread or toast instead of jam. Cut into the toast into fingers to make it easy for little ones to eat.

 rice cakes with fruit dip

5 cherries, stoned
1 tbsp thick apple purée
2 plain unsalted rice cakes or corn cakes

Finely chop or mash the cherries and put into a bowl. Add the apple purée. Serve as a dip with the rice cakes. Babies also love eating cherries, but of course make sure you remove the stones and halve them first.

 bacon and mushrooms nibbles

1 rasher unsmoked streaky bacon or pancetta
4 button mushrooms
4 cocktail sticks

Remove the rind from the bacon – you don't need to with pancetta – and cut into four. Wrap each piece around a mushroom and push onto a cocktail stick. Bake in a medium oven, or grill, until the bacon is just crisp and cooked. Finely chop or lightly mash if necessary.

 **cucumber sticks with mint dip**

¼ cucumber peeled
2 tbsp natural full-fat yogurt
1 tbsp full-fat cream cheese
1–2 mint leaves, finely chopped.

Cut the cucumber into 1cm sticks. Mix the yogurt, cheese, and mint together. Encourage your baby to dip the cucumber sticks into the minty yogurt to help him improve his coordination.

 **malt loaf with mashed bananas**

¼ ripe large banana, peeled and mashed
1 slice malt loaf

Spread the banana on the malt loaf and cut into bite-sized piece. Malt loaf is quite high in sugar, so don't indulge them with this too often.

2 2 1½ 16½

hot tuna toasts

4 tbsp tinned tuna in oil,
drained and flaked
25g Cheddar cheese, grated
1 tsp natural full-fat yogurt
1 piece wholemeal bread

Mix the tuna, cheese, and yogurt together. Spread onto the bread and cook under a medium grill until the top is golden and bubbling. Cut into finger-size pieces. Add a little finely chopped parsley or ripe avocado if you have any to hand.

2½ **C** ½ 1

fruit with prune purée

6 ready-to-eat prunes
a little apple juice
½ ripe medium banana, peeled and
cut into chunks

Heat the prunes in a small pan with the apple juice until they soften (approximately 5 minutes). Whiz them in a blender until smooth. Serve with chunks of banana, or any other soft fruit to dip into the purée.

½ **C** 1 ½ 1 4½

soft flour tortillas with avocado

2 tbsp full-fat cream cheese
1 soft flour tortilla
¼ ripe avocado, mashed

Spread the cream cheese onto the tortilla, then top with the mashed avocado. Roll up the tortilla and cut into fine slices for your baby to nibble on. Add a little finely chopped fresh coriander to make it more zingy if you have some.

2 **C** 2 1 1 5½

dried fruits with vanilla yogurt

small handful of dried fruit, eg apple
or pear, finely chopped
50ml apple juice
2cm piece of vanilla pod
100ml natural full-fat yogurt

Put the fruit to soak in the apple juice for at least half an hour. Slice the piece of vanilla pod in half, scrape the seeds into the yogurt and mix well. Mix the dried fruit into the yogurt and serve.

2½ **C** ½ ½ 4½

cottage cheese and pineapple

3 tbsp full-fat cottage cheese
1–2 mint leaves, finely chopped
100g fresh pineapple, peeled and
cut into big chunks

Mash the cottage cheese really well with the mint. Serve as a dip with the pineapple. You can leave the mint out and add a little crumbled cooked bacon or chicken instead if you prefer.

½ **C** ½ ½ ½ 5

steamed vegetables with cottage cheese

3 tbsp full-fat cottage cheese
1 tsp fresh parsley, finely chopped
handful of steamed vegetable sticks
eg carrots, courgettes, asparagus

Mash the cottage cheese with the parsley and serve as a dip with the steamed vegetables. You could serve the vegetables with hummus instead of the cheese.

All quick bites make 1 portion
unless otherwise stated.

quick bites snacks

  ½ ½ 9½
Vitamin B₁₂

pasta with pesto and tuna

75g cooked pasta
1 tsp pesto
30g tinned tuna in oil, drained and flaked

Mix everything together while the pasta is still hot and then finely chop. This works just as well with chopped cooked chicken instead of the tuna.

2½   ½ 1 1 4½

cheesy peas

2 tbsp full-fat cream cheese
100g frozen peas, freshly cooked

Add the cream cheese to the peas while they are still hot, mash slightly, and stir well. Add some chopped fresh herbs, such as parsley, if you have any.

½ ½ 1 1 3½

cream cheese and beetroot soldiers

1 tbsp full-fat cream cheese
1 piece wholemeal bread
50g cooked beetroot, finely chopped

Spread the cream cheese on the bread and top with the beetroot. Cut into little soldiers.

---

1   2 ½ 16½

coronation chicken

75g cooked chicken, finely chopped
2 tbsp natural full-fat yogurt
1 tsp mango chutney, chopped

Mix all the ingredients together and serve with 50g finely chopped cooked, cooled rice or pasta.

---

 3 2 1½ 10
Vitamin B₁₂

sardines on toast

1 piece of brown toast
knob of unsalted butter
2 tinned boned sardines, mashed
freshly ground black pepper

Spread the toast with the butter and top with the mashed sardines. Grill until hot through and slice before serving with a pinch of ground black pepper.

1½ **C** ½ 1

apricots with cream cheese

4 dried apricots
50ml apple juice
1 tbsp full-fat cream cheese

Leave the apricots to soak in the apple juice for at least half an hour. Finely chop the apricots and mix with the cream cheese. You can add a little ground cinnamon to the cream cheese to make it more interesting.

tarragon chicken with wholemeal bread

75g cooked chicken, finely chopped
2 tbsp natural full-fat yogurt
pinch fresh tarragon, finely chopped
1 slice wholemeal bread, chopped
1 ripe tomato, finely chopped

Mix the finely chopped cooked chicken with the yogurt and fresh tarragon and then stir well. Serve with the small pieces of fresh bread and finely chopped ripe tomato.

bagels with ham and mozzarella

½ bagel
50g cooked ham, chopped
50g full-fat mozzarella cheese, grated
ripe avocado, peeled

Toast the bagel, top with the ham and cheese, then grill until the mozzarella is bubbling and golden. Slice before serving with some mashed avocado.

pasta with creamy tomato sauce

50ml tomato passata
75g pasta, freshly cooked
1 tbsp full-fat cream cheese

Heat the tomato passata in a pan, add the pasta, and stir well until heated through. Add the cream cheese. If necessary, finely chop before serving.

courgette and cottage cheese

1 small courgette, grated
1 tbsp olive oil, for frying
50g full-fat cottage cheese
freshly ground black pepper
1 tsp finely chopped parsley

Fry the courgette in the oil until just cooked. Stir in the cottage cheese. Add some freshly ground black pepper and the finely chopped parsley, and serve with pieces of brown bread.

Vitamin B₁

couscous with ham and tomato

50g couscous, cooked
30g cooked ham, chopped
1 tomato, finely chopped
freshly ground black pepper
1 tsp fresh herbs, eg parsley, finely chopped

Mix the couscous, ham and tomato together, then season with freshly ground black pepper and finely chopped herbs. Finely chop before serving.

Vitamin B₁

pasta with courgette and bacon

75g pasta, freshly cooked
50g courgette, cooked and grated
5 tbsp tomato passata
1 rasher unsmoked streaky bacon, cooked and finely chopped

Mix all the ingredients together in the pan that the pasta was cooked in and heat gently until the sauce is hot. Finely chop before serving.

All quick bites make 1 portion
unless otherwise stated.

fresh puddings

cocoa rice pudding

3½

½

½

½

Vitamin B₁₂

makes: 5 baby portions or 1 baby portions and 2 adult portions

storage: rice should never be reheated, but can be served cold up to 24 hours after cooking

250ml full-fat milk or soya drink

250ml coconut milk

100ml water

2 tsp good cocoa powder

2 tsp golden caster sugar (or preferably omit)

½ tsp vanilla extract

150g short-grain pudding rice

little knob of unsalted butter

There are many variations of this recipe – why not try making a plain vanilla rice pudding, by omitting the cocoa and adding a split vanilla pod with the milk and water, and then swirling in some apple or banana purée? Do not serve coconut to babies if there is a family history of allergies.

1 Put the milk, coconut milk and water into a saucepan and bring the mixture up to the boil.

2 Put the cocoa in a bowl with the sugar (if using) and vanilla extract. Pour the hot milk over the cocoa mixture, stirring constantly. Pour back into the saucepan

3 Add the rice and bring back to the boil. Reduce the heat and simmer for 15 to 20 minutes, stirring often to prevent the mixture from sticking on the bottom of the pan.

4 If necessary, add a few tablespoons of water in order to loosen the mixture a little.

5 Add butter, mix well and cook for 1 more minute.

tropical fruits with raspberry sauce

1

makes: 2 baby portions

storage: up to 24 hours in the refrigerator

½ ripe medium papaya

¼ small ripe melon

4 tbsp fresh orange juice

100g raspberries

Note: babies develop at different rates; do not feed chopped food to your baby until he is confident with chewing.

This is a brilliant way to encourage babies to eat fruit – not that most need much encouragement. You can make this quick and simple sauce out of lots of soft fruits; try strawberries or blueberries instead of raspberries.

1 Scoop the seeds out of the papaya and peel and cut the flesh into very small pieces. Peel the melon, removing any pips, and cut into very small pieces.

2 Put the papaya and melon into a bowl with 2 tbsp orange juice and mix gently.

3 Push the raspberries through a nylon sieve, scraping the bottom well. Mix with the remaining orange juice.

4 Serve half the fruit in a small bowl with half the raspberry sauce drizzled over it. Mash the fruits a little if your baby will find it easier.

raspberry and mango soup

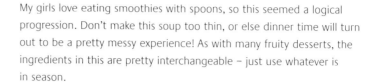

½

½

9½ **C**

Vitamin A

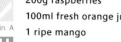

makes: 3 baby portions or
1 baby portion and 1 adult
portion

storage: up to 24 hours in the
refrigerator

200g raspberries
100ml fresh orange juice
1 ripe mango

My girls love eating smoothies with spoons, so this seemed a logical
progression. Don't make this soup too thin, or else dinner time will turn
out to be a pretty messy experience! As with many fruity desserts, the
ingredients in this are pretty interchangeable – just use whatever is
in season.

1 Whiz the raspberries and orange juice in a hand-held blender (or food
processor or blender) until smooth.

2 Slice the mango down either side of the stone and peel the skin from the
flesh.

3 Cut the mango into small pieces, then mash with a fork until it is just lumpy.
Mix in the raspberry purée.

fruit trifle

3½

½

½

1

5 **C**

makes: 3 baby portions or
1 baby portion and 1 adult
portion

storage: up to 24 hours in the
refrigerator

200g mixed soft fruit,
  eg raspberries, strawberries,
  blueberries, fresh or frozen
2 tbsp fresh orange juice
4 sponge fingers
150ml natural full-fat yogurt

This is really quick and easy. If you have any leftover muffin or fruit loaf you
can use that instead of sponge fingers. Equally, you can use custard (see page
124) instead of yogurt.

1 Put the fruit and orange juice in a pan and heat gently until the fruits begin
to burst. Lightly mash.

2 Arrange the sponge fingers in a small dish and spoon over three-quarters of
the warm fruit. Leave to soak for at least 30 minutes. Lightly mash if necessary.

3 Gently swirl the remaining fruit through the yogurt and pour over the fruits
and sponge.

vanilla pears

makes 3–4 baby portions or 1 baby portion and 1 adult portion

storage up to 24 hours in the refrigerator s

2 ripe pears, eg Williams
1 tsp soft brown sugar
1 tbsp lemon juice
1 vanilla pod, sliced
  lengthways (optional)
small knob of unsalted
  butter
natural full-fat yogurt

This is a really delicious wintry pudding, especially if you add a little pinch of ground ginger. If you have any left over, it's also very good cold served with yogurt or muesli for breakfast.

1 Preheat the oven to 180°C/350°F/gas mark 4.
2 Peel the pears with a sharp knife or peeler and then core them before cutting them into thin slices.
3 Put the pears in an ovenproof dish and then toss them with the sugar, lemon juice, vanilla pod and butter.
4 Bake the pears for approximately 20 minutes, basting occasionally, until tender and golden.
5 To serve, remove the vanilla pod and finely chop or mash the pears.

baked bananas with raspberries

makes: 1 baby portion
storage: best eaten immediately

1 medium ripe banana
handful of raspberries
  (optional)
pinch of ground cinnamon
  (optional)
3 tbsp fresh orange juice

Bananas are always popular with babies. Baking intensifies their flavour and makes them even more irresistible. Bananas can be baked whole, in their skins; just cook them on a baking tray and let them cool before opening. They are also great mashed with natural full-fat yogurt.

1 Preheat the oven to 180°C/350°F/gas mark 4.
2 Lightly butter an ovenproof dish.
3 Peel the banana and slice in half lengthways.
4 Put the banana into the dish and sprinkle with the raspberries and cinnamon, if using. Pour over the orange juice.
5 Bake in the oven for 20 minutes, until soft. Cool slightly and finely chop or mash before serving.

quick bites puddings

fruit with cinnamon cream cheese

small selection of soft fruit, eg banana,
¼ mango, ¼ peach
20g full-fat cream cheese
pinch of ground cinnamon

Peel the banana and mango. Beat the cream cheese with the cinnamon until smooth. Cut the fruit into slices and serve with the cheese as a dip or, if your baby is less confident with chewing, finely chop the fruit and mix into the cheese.

banana baked with apricots

½ small ripe banana, peeled
2–3 tinned apricots halves
small knob of unsalted butter

Put the fruit into a small baking dish and dot with the butter. Cover with foil and bake in a preheated oven at 180°C/350°F/gas mark 4 until the fruit is soft. Cool. Mash lightly before serving.

autumn rice pudding

1/2 small ripe pear, peeled, cored and chopped
pinch ground cinnamon
100g rice pudding (see page 182)

Simmer the pear in 2tbsp water until soft. Stir the pear and cinnamon into the rice pudding just before serving.

rice pudding with dried fruit purée

30g dried fruits, eg raisins, dates and prunes, finely chopped
50ml apple juice
100g rice pudding (see page 182)

Heat the dried fruit and apple juice together in a pan for 5-10 minutes, then leave to stand for at least 10 minutes. Beat into a purée. Stir into the rice pudding just before serving.

baked almond peach

1 ripe peach, halved and stoned
1 tbsp ground almonds
small knob of unsalted butter

Put the peach in a roasting dish, sprinkle with the ground almonds and dot with the butter. Bake in a medium oven until soft and golden (5 minutes). Finely chop. Do not feed nuts to babies if there is any family history of allergies.

Vitamin B₁₂
nutty fruit yogurt

1 tbsp dried fruits, eg dates,
raisins and apricots, finely chopped
100g natural full-fat yogurt
1 tbsp ground nuts

Heat the dried fruit in a pan with 1-2 tbsp water for 5-10 minutes, then leave to stand for at least 10 minutes. Beat into a purée. Mix all the ingredients together and leave to sit for 5 minutes. Do not feed nuts to babies if there is any family history of allergies.

strawberries with passion fruit

12 **C** ½ 🥚

75g strawberries, hulled
1 passion fruit

Roughly mash the strawberries. Cut the passion fruit in half and scrape the flesh out over the strawberries.

apple and cheddar crackers

½ **C** 2 🥛 1 ½ 🐟 6 🥚

4 tbsp apple purée (see page 78)
30g Cheddar cheese, finely diced
1-2 oat crackers

Serve the apple purée and cheese dice with the crackers. Only serve this to babies who are very confident with chewing.

apple purée with raisin toast

1 **C** ½ 🥛 ½ 🐟 2½ 🥚

1 slice of raisin bread, lightly toasted
60g natural full-fat yogurt
4 tbsp apple purée (see page 78)

Break up the toast into tiny pieces and stir into the yogurt. Leave to soak for a few minutes, then swirl through the apple purée.

raisin bread with stewed fruit

✓ 1 **C**

Vitamin B₁, B₁₂, A

1 slice raisin bread
50ml full-fat milk
50g stewed fruit, eg plums

Tear the bread into tiny pieces and leave to soak in the milk for a few minutes. Stir the stewed plums into the mixture just before serving. Mash if necessary.

melon with passion fruit yogurt

3 **C** 1 🥛 ½ 🐟 2½ 🥚

1 passion fruit, halved
50g natural full-fat yogurt
75g fresh ripe melon, cut into tiny chunks

Mix the passion fruit flesh into the yogurt. Serve the mixture as a dip with the melon chunks.

baby muesli bar with yogurt

✓ 1 🥛 1½ 🐟 1 6 🥚

Vitamin B₁

1 baby muesli bar
50g natural full-fat yogurt

Break tiny pieces of the muesli bar into the yogurt. If you like, add a few drops of vanilla extract.

All quick bites make 1 portion unless otherwise stated.

puddings to freeze

berry sponge

makes: 10 baby portions

storage: up to 3 months in the freezer

125g unsalted butter, softened
75g golden caster sugar
2 eggs, lightly beaten
2 drops vanilla extract
125g self-raising flour
175g mixed berries, eg blueberries, raspberries, cherries (stoned), fresh or frozen

If you can't get hold of any fresh berries, use a bag of the frozen forest fruits or summer berries instead. You can add the berries to the sponge mixture while they are still frozen.

1 Preheat oven to 180°C/350°F/gas mark 4. Grease a deep 20cm round or square cake tin.
2 Beat together the butter and sugar until soft and fluffy. Gradually add the eggs, beating well. You may need to add a little flour to stop the mixture from curdling.
3 Beat in the vanilla extract, then fold in the flour. Add the berries and gently stir to mix through.
4 Spoon the mixture into the prepared tin. Bake for 25-30 minutes, until golden on top and spongy to touch.
5 Leave to cool in the tin for a few minutes before transferring to a cooling rack.
6 When cool, wrap up in foil and freeze or cut into slices and freeze individually.
7 To serve, defrost thoroughly and then mash or finely chop.

banana and apple crumble

makes: 6 baby portions

storage: up to 3 months in the freezer

3 medium cooking apples
juice and zest of 1 orange
1 tsp soft brown sugar
100g plain flour
50g unsalted butter
50g porridge oats
2 tsp golden caster sugar
pinch of ground cinnamon
2 small ripe bananas, peeled and finely chopped

Vitamin B₁

Note: do not feed chopped food to your baby until he is confident with chewing.

Any fruits can be used in crumbles. Using bananas means that you can keep the amount of added sugar to a minimum, which is definitely no bad thing.

1 Peel, core and thinly slice the apples. Put them into a pan with the orange juice, zest, and brown sugar. Heat gently until the apples are slightly soft – approximately 10 minutes.
2 Sieve the flour into a bowl and rub in the butter until the mixture resembles breadcrumbs. Stir in the oats, caster sugar, and cinnamon.
3 Put the fruit into a dish or into small ramekins and sprinkle over the crumble mixture.
4 Leave to cool, wrap in foil, and freeze.
5 To serve, thaw thoroughly. Preheat the oven to 180°C/350°F/gas mark 4. Bake in the oven for 25 minutes, until the crumble is crisp and golden.
6 To serve, mash or finely chop.

apple flapjacks

makes: 15 baby portions

storage: up to 3 months in the freezer

125g unsalted butter
75g soft brown sugar
2 tbsp golden syrup
350g porridge oats
½ tsp baking powder
2 eating apples, peeled,
  cored and grated
50g hazelnuts, toasted and
  ground

These are great flapjacks because they are soft, moist, and slightly crumbly, rather than hard and chewy, which can be too much for many babies. The apple gives a natural sweetness so these flapjacks are not as sugar-laden as many shop-bought ones. Do not feed nuts to babies if there is any family history of allergies.

1 Preheat the oven to 180°C/350°F/gas mark 4. Grease a 23cm x 33cm Swiss roll tin.

2 Melt the butter, sugar, and golden syrup together in a large saucepan over a low heat.

3 In a bowl, mix together the oats, baking powder, apples, and ground hazelnuts, stirring well. Then add to the butter mixture and mix together.

4 Tip into the tin and flatten the surface. Bake for 20 minutes, until the edges are just beginning to turn golden. Cut into squares while still warm and leave to cool in the tin.

5 Layer with greaseproof paper and store in freezer bags. Freeze.

6 To serve, thaw thoroughly and chop into very small pieces.

scones

makes: 8 baby portions

storage: up to 3 months in the freezer

225g self-raising flour
1 tbsp sugar
1 level tsp baking powder
50g butter
100ml milk, plus a little
  extra for brushing

These make eight standard-sized scones, but if you think your baby will only manage half, just make them smaller!

1 Preheat the oven to 230°C/450°F/gas mark 8. Sieve the flour, sugar and baking powder into a bowl and then rub in the butter until the mixture resembles breadcrumbs.

2 Make a well in the centre, stir in the milk, and bring together to form a soft dough.

3 Turn the mixture out onto a floured surface and knead very lightly. Roll out until about 2cm thick. Cut out eight rounds with a cutter.

4 Put the scones on to a baking sheet and brush with milk. Bake for 8-10 minutes, until golden brown and well-risen.

5 Leave to cool, freeze in an airtight container.

6 To serve, thaw thoroughly and then chop into very small pieces.

banana custard

½

Vitamin B₁₂

1+

makes: 10 baby portions

storage: up to 3 months in the freezer

200ml full-fat milk or
    calcium-enriched soya drink
1 vanilla pod, split
    lengthways
3 large free-range egg yolks
1 tsp golden caster sugar
1 tbsp cornflour
2 medium ripe bananas
100g natural Greek yogurt

Bananas are a perennially popular food for babies, although you can try this recipe with mango instead of banana if you prefer.

1 To make the custard, heat the milk with the vanilla pod in a saucepan until just below boiling point. Remove from heat and take out the vanilla pod

2 In a bowl, mix the egg yolks, sugar, and cornflour together. Pour the hot milk over the egg mixture, stirring constantly until smooth.

3 Return to the saucepan and heat, stirring constantly, until the mixture thickens. Do not allow to boil or it will curdle.

4 Once the custard has thickened, leave it to cool.

5 Meanwhile, purée the bananas and yogurt together in a bowl with a hand-held blender (or in a food processor or blender). Gently fold together the cooled custard and bananas mixture. Remove the vanilla pod.

6 Spoon the purée into ice-cube trays. Cover with foil or put into a freezer bag and seal. Freeze for at least four hours, until frozen. Transfer to freezer bags and return to the freezer.

7 To serve, thaw thoroughly. Heat gently until warm.

stewed plums

½

3 C

makes: 4 baby portions or 2 baby portions and 1 adult portion

storage: up to 3 months in the freezer

12 ripe plums
juice of 2 oranges
pinch of ground cinnamon
1-2 tsp soft brown sugar,
    (optional – add to taste)

The plums must be ripe for this to be tasty without you having to add too much sugar. These stewed plums are great added to yogurt for a quick pudding, used as the base for a crumble, or even added to cereals for either pudding or breakfast.

1 Cut the plums in half, remove the stones, and slice. Put the fruit into a saucepan, then add the orange juice and cinnamon.

2 Bring up to the boil, reduce the heat and simmer gently for 5-8 minutes, depending on the plums' ripeness, until they are lovely and soft in a sweet syrup. Add a little sugar if they are too tart.

3 Spoon the plums into ice-cube trays. Cover with foil or put into a freezer bag and seal. Freeze. When frozen, transfer to freezer bags and return to the freezer.

4 To serve, thaw thoroughly. Heat the plums gently until warm and the lightly mash if necessary.

Index

additives, artificial 23-5, 89
alcohol 37
allergies 11, 22, 25, 44, 66, 89, 90, 136, 138
almonds, ground 87
antioxidants 13, 19, 25
apricots 88
asthma 22, 25, 89, 136
avocados 26, 27

babies
    digestive system 10, 18, 23-4, 88-90, 94, 135, 138
    essential nutrients 10-11, 21, 25
    immune system 10, 13, 18, 20, 23, 87, 89
    nervous system 18, 19, 23
    nocturnal feeders 37
    premature 47
bananas 24, 26, 277
beaker/feeder cup 92, 134-7
beans 88, 90, 135
behavioural problems 25
betacarotene 18
bloating 90, 138
blood
    calcium and 14
    high blood pressure 90, 138
    iron and 15
    vitamin B and 18
    vitamin E and 19
boiled food 27
boiled water
    between feeds/meals 27, 36, 46, 89, 90, 91, 93,137, 142
    diluting mid-morning feed 136
bones, nutrients for 14, 19
bottles
    bottle-feeding 23, 37
    sterilizing 29
    weaning from 137
botulism 44, 90, 138
bowel movements 93, 135, 138
bread 89, 135, 136
    wholemeal 89, 90, 135, 138
breast milk 15, 16, 18, 19, 20-3
    freezing 27, 34
    mixed with purées 44, 66, 78
    nutrients 15, 16, 18, 19, 21, 41, 45, 87, 91, 135
    sterilizing 28-9
breast-feeding 10, 20-3
    0-3 months 31-7
    change to bottle-feeding 47
    diet when 22, 23, 37
    expressing milk 23, 34, 35, 36
    organic 22, 23
    painful 37, 43
    pesticide residues and 23
    reducing milk intake 136, 139
    routine 33-6, 46, 91, 92
    vegan and vegetarian diets 18
breast-pumps 34
broccoli 88

cabbage leaves 37
caffeine 15, 37, 44, 90, 138
calcium 7, 14, 41
    vegan & vegetarian sources 87
carbohydrates 16, 17, 87, 135
carrots 27, 137
cereals 135
    breakfast 88
    sugar-free unrefined 90, 136
charts, how to use 6-7
cheese 44, 90, 138
chickpeas 90
coeliac disease 44
coffee 37, 44, 90, 138
colic 37
colostrum 20, 33-4
constipation 93, 139
crying 47, 136, 9

dehydration 44, 90, 93, 138
diabetes 90, 135
diarrhoea 22, 90, 138

eating utensils
    sterilizing 89
    washing and drying 29, 137
eczema 22, 25, 89
eggs 12, 135, 138
    dangers from 44, 90, 138
energy 16, 17, 135, 136
engorged breasts 37, 43
enzymes, and babies health 11, 20
essential fatty acids 16, 22

fat
    for strength 139
    low-fat diet myth 89
    saturated/unsaturated 16, 22, 137
fatty foods 44
feeding
    eating problems 47, 141
    a full baby 93
fibre 17, 88-9, 135, 138
fish 12, 16, 44, 88, 90, 138
foods
    additives 23, 24, 25, 89
    at 4-6 months 44-5
    at 7-9 months 90-1
    at 10-12 months 138-9
    convenience foods 26
    freezing 27, 34
    freshness 25-6
    irradiation and 24
    organic 22, 23, 24, 90
    pesticide residues 23, 24, 89
    preservatives 24, 25
    seasonal 24
    spicy 44, 90, 134, 138
    volume at 4-6 months 45
    volume at 7-9 months 91
    volume at 10-12 months 139
formula milk 20, 22, 23, 32
    fat and energy 16
    nutrients 15, 18, 19, 21, 41, 45, 91, 135

organic 23
    sterilizing 28-9
fruit
    citrus 37, 44, 90
    dried 88, 90, 136
    fibre source 135, 138
    juices 23, 137
    purées 27, 46, 137
    steamed and boiled 27
frustration, when eating 47

garlic 37
genetically modified (GM) foods 23, 24-5
gluten 44
golden syrup 90, 138

herbs 137
honey 26, 44, 90
hygiene 28-9, 89
hyperactivity, food colourings 25

iodine 87
iron 7, 15, 87, 88
    absorption 15, 44, 90, 138
    vegans and vegetarians 87, 88
irradiation, of foods 24

kitchen, hygiene/equipment 28-9

labelling 25-7, 89, 90, 138
lentils 90
listeria 44, 90, 138

margarine, vegan 87
marmite 90, 138
mastitis 43
meal planners
    4-6 months 48-9
    7-9 months 94-5
    10-12 months 142-3
meals, planning 7
mealtimes 93
    a full baby 93
    participation in family meals 86, 93, 133, 134, 137, 139
meat
    nutritional source 12, 135
    unprocessed 24
    weaning and 88, 90
microwaving 27
milk and dairy foods
    allergies 44, 89
    cow's milk 22-4, 89, 90, 138
    follow-on milk 23
    full-fat 18, 89, 90, 135, 138
    goat's milk 23
    key nutrients 41
    organic 90
    pesticide residues 24, 90
    sheep's milk 23
    unsuitability of for babies 23, 90
mothers, routine with babies 33-6, 46, 91, 92,140

National Childbirth Trust 23
nut butters 90

nutrients required per day
charts 7
    4-6 months 41
    7-9 months 87
    10-12 months 135
nutrition 9-26
    essential nutrients 10-11
    for immunity 41, 139
    for strength 139
    vegetarian and vegan 87, 135
nuts 22, 87, 90, 102, 136
    allergies 44, 89, 136, 138

obesity 90, 135
oils 16, 22, 87
onions 37

pasta 89, 90
peanut allergies 44, 138
peas 88, 135, 137, 138
pesticides 23, 24
phosphorus 19
poultry 88, 90, 135
premature babies 47
protein 12, 87, 88, 135, 139
    meal planning 7, 94, 138
    sources of 12, 135, 136
    vegan and vegetarian sources 12, 87, 135, 136, 138
pulses 88, 90, 135

rashes 22
riboflavin 87
rice
    baby rice 24, 44, 55, 66, 78
    brown rice 135, 138
    rice cakes 89
    rice starch 26
routines
    breast-feeding 33-6, 46, 91, 92, 140
    meal times 139, 140
    for solid foods 91, 92, 140

salmonella 90
salt 26, 44, 89, 90, 137, 138
seeds 87
self-feeding 86, 92, 93, 133, 134, 136-7, 141
shellfish 44, 90, 138
sleep
    for baby 34-6, 46, 92, 140
    for mother 33
soya products 23
spices 137
starch 17, 26, 139
steamed food 27

stock cubes 90, 138
sugars 17, 26, 44, 89, 90, 135, 137, 138, 139
sunlight 19, 87
sweeteners, artificial 90, 138

tannins 15, 44, 90, 138
tantrums, food colouring and 25
tea 37, 44, 90, 138
teeth 88, 137
    development nutrients 14, 19
    tooth decay 44, 90, 135, 137, 138
teething 40, 93, 94, 136
tiredness, when breast-feeding 34
tofu 135
tomatoes, finger food 137
treacle 90, 138

vegan and vegetarian diets 18, 87, 135
    vitamin B2 deficiency 18
    zinc deficiency 14
vegetable extracts 26
vegetables 11, 27, 87-8
    juices 135, 138
    pesticide residues 24
    purées 27, 46
vitamins 11
    vitamin A 16, 18, 41
    vitamin B vitamins 18
    vitamin B_2 (riboflavin) 87
    vitamin C 7, 13, 41, 94
    vitamin D 16, 19, 22, 87
    vitamin E 16, 19, 41
    vitamin K 16
    supplements 18, 19, 22
vomiting 22

water see boiled water
watercress 88
weaning 11, 15, 18, 23
    4-6 months 39, 40-7
    7-9 months 87, 88-93
    10-12 months 136-41
weight gain 32, 35, 39
weight loss 32
wheat products 24, 44, 87, 89, 90
    see also cereals
wheat starch 26
wholegrain 135
wind 90, 138

yeast extracts 90, 138
yogurt 90

zinc 7, 14, 41

Thanks to the babies…

Particular thanks to Abraham, Anna, Archie, Ava, Ben, Ella, Elysia, Finn, Flynn, Hetty, Jamal, Jasmine, Kieran, Martha, Mae, Oliver and Phoebe for smiling for the camera and eating up all the food I cooked.